I0426151

May 2002

INTEGRATION OF ENVIRONMENTAL JUSTICE IN FEDERAL AGENCY PROGRAMS

A Report developed from the National Environmental Justice Advisory Council Meeting of December 11-14, 2000

NATIONAL ENVIRONMENTAL JUSTICE ADVISORY COUNCIL

A Federal Advisory Committee to the U. S. Environmental Protection Agency

 **NATIONAL ENVIRONMENTAL JUSTICE ADVISORY COUNCIL**

June 25, 2002

Administrator Christine Todd Whitman
U.S. Environmental Protection Agency
1200 Pennsylvania Avenue, NW
Washington, DC 20004

Dear Administrator Whitman:

Please find attached a copy of the report entitled "**National Environmental Justice Advisory Council's Report on Integration of Environmental Justice in Federal Agency Programs, May 2002.**"

EPA, through its Office of Environmental Justice, requested the National Environmental Justice Advisory Council (NEJAC) in its meeting of December 11 - 14, 2000 to provide advice and recommendations on federal government efforts toward integrating environmental justice into agency policies, programs, and activities consistent with the existing laws and Executive Order (E.O.) 1998. The NEJAC believes that this report has special significance for the EPA. EPA chairs the Interagency Working Group on Environmental Justice (IWG), which was established by E.O. 12898.

In short, this report reflects the advice and recommendations that resulted from pre-meeting preparation (i.e., interviews), on-site discussions, public comments and subsequent analysis. The breath of the discussions is exemplified by individuals and/or organizations that either provided comments, suggestions or recommendations on the importance of interagency strategies and coordination for achieving environmental justice across the federal family.

This report proposes five overarching recommendations to the EPA as follows:

(1) Support advancement of the Interagency Working Group (IWG) on Environmental Justice Action Agenda and its collaborative interagency problem-solving model as exemplified in the fifteen demonstration projects.

(2) Continue individual agency-specific implementation of environmental justice.

(3) Explore and identify ways for greater use of legal authorities and removal of regulatory impediments to achieve environmental justice.

A Federal Advisory Committee to the U.S. Environmental Protection Agency

(4) Ensure that, in the case of federally-recognized tribes including Alaska Native villages, integration of environmental justice into agency policies, programs, and activities is consistent with federal trust responsibility to tribes, recognized principles of tribal sovereignty, and the government-to-government relationship with tribes.

(5) Collaborate in identifying specific focus areas or target programs where application of environmental justice principles could significantly benefit communities.

The NEJAC is pleased to present this report to you for your review, consideration, response and action. In addition, we request that you forward this report to your counterparts with other relevant federal agencies.

Sincerely,

Peggy M. Shepard
Chair

TABLE OF CONTENTS

1. INTRODUCTION

This document provides an analysis of the information presented at the December 11-14, 2000 NEJAC meeting. The purpose of the meeting was to present information on federal government progress integrating environmental justice into agency policies, programs, and activities consistent with existing laws and the Executive Order No. 12898, "Federal Actions to Address Environmental Justice in Minority Populations and Low-Income Populations." The December 2000 meeting was informative and provided an excellent opportunity for federal agencies and stakeholders to identify areas for furtherance of environmental justice principles throughout their endeavors and programs. The recommendations of this report may appear somewhat broad in scope, but they set the groundwork for future more detailed review and evaluation by the various federal agencies as they pursue substantive areas which may involve multi-agency participation.

As a result of the meeting, the NEJAC proposes five overarching recommendations. Under each general recommendation, the Council proposes more specific recommendations. Although both the general and specific recommendations appear at the conclusion of the report, the five overarching recommendations are that the EPA and other federal agencies should:

1. Support advancement of the Interagency Working Group (IWG) on Environmental Justice Action Agenda and its collaborative interagency problem-solving model as exemplified in the fifteen demonstration projects;

2. Continue individual agency-specific implementation of environmental justice;

3. Explore and identify ways for greater use of legal authorities and removal of regulatory impediments to achieve environmental justice;

4. Ensure that, in the case of federally-recognized tribes including Alaska Native villages, integration of environmental justice into agency policies, programs, and activities is consistent with the federal trust responsibility to tribes, recognized principles of tribal sovereignty, and the government-to-government relationship with tribes. More specifically, NEJAC incorporates by reference the further recommendations specific to tribes and Indian country developed by its Indigenous Peoples Subcommittee and attached hereto as Appendix A; and

5. Collaborate in identifying specific focus areas or target programs where application of environmental justice principles could significantly benefit communities.

The sections below present the information from the meeting that support these recommendations. This report is organized as follows:

- Section 2, "Statutory Basis for Environmental Justice," discusses the need for environmental justice statutory authorities and describes how existing statutes can be used to support environmental justice activities.

- Section 3, "Analysis of Progress in Federal Agency Implementation," discusses federal agency progress in implementing the mission of the EO, within the context of a general framework.

- Section 4, "Interagency Collaboration," summarizes specific agency accomplishments in interagency collaboration, based on NEJAC presentations.

- Section 5," Conclusions and Recommendations," summarizes the document.

2.   STATUTORY BASIS FOR ENVIRONMENTAL JUSTICE

The purpose of the December 2000 NEJAC meeting was to examine federal agency progress in integrating environmental justice into agency operations, *consistent with existing laws and the Executive Order.* Therefore, one of the issues to be examined is the extent to which agencies have and are able to use existing laws to address environmental justice concerns that may arise in their day-to-day operations.

Executive Order 12898, "Federal Actions to Address Environmental Justice in Minority Populations and Low-Income Populations," directs EPA and other federal agencies to make environmental justice part of their mission.   However, the EO does not provide a statutory basis for taking actions based on environmental justice concerns. The purpose of this section is to examine the potential for using existing statutes and regulations to address environmental justice concerns and explore the need for the development of new authorities.

2.1   Potential for Using Existing Statutes

The environmental statutes and regulations implemented by EPA and used by other agencies provide broadly worded language and grant discretionary authority that can be used to address environmental justice issues. For example, the requirements for implementing the National Environmental Policy Act (NEPA)[1] make clear that environmental justice concerns should be considered as part of the NEPA process. Under the regulations implementing NEPA, agencies must analyze "ecological, aesthetic, historical, cultural, economic, or health [impacts]; whether direct, indirect, or cumulative,"[2] when preparing environmental assessments (EAs) and environmental impact statements (EISs) required by the law. The analyses required under NEPA can be useful tools for identifying potential concerns or issues affecting low-income and/or minority communities. Furthermore, under NEPA, agencies must evaluate and consider mitigation of significant adverse environmental effects on minority and/or low-income communities.

In addition to NEPA, other environmental statutes are available to address environmental justice concerns. At the December NEJAC meeting, Mr. Tony Guadagno (Office of General Counsel, EPA) identified opportunities to promote environmental justice under EPA permitting programs. His presentation was based on a memorandum issued by Mr. Gary Guzy (General Counsel) that specifically reviewed permitting under the Clean Water Act (CWA), the Clean Air Act (CAA), the Resource Conservation and Recovery Act (RCRA), the Safe Drinking Water Act (SDWA), and Title I of the Marine Protection, Research, and Sanctuaries Act.[3] The Guzy memorandum suggests that the use of EPA's statutory authorities under these acts may, in some cases, require the modification or issuance of guidance documents, interpretive rules, or substantive rules. The language in these acts, coupled with discretionary authority under existing agency regulations, could allow EPA to include strong environmental justice concerns in its permitting process. Mr. Guadagno did not provide any details of the

---

[1] National Environmental Policy Act, 42 U.S.C. Section 4321.

[2] 40 C.F.R. Section 1508.8.

[3]

Memorandum from Gary S. Guzy, Office of General Counsel, to Steven A. Herman, Office of Enforcement and Compliance Monitoring, regarding "EPA Statutory and Regulatory Authorities Under Which Environmental Justice Issues May be Addressed in Permitting" distributed to the NEJAC on December 1, 2000.

memorandum in his presentation. However, the section below presents examples of some of the statutory provisions that illustrate the potential for using existing statutes to promote environmental justice. These examples are based on the Guzy memorandum as well as previous research on this subject, such as that conducted by Professor Richard Lazarus and others on behalf of the NEJAC subcommittee, which was subsequently presented in an article authored by Professor Lazarus and Dr. Stephanie Tai.[4]

Clean Air Act (CAA)

Multiple authorities within the CAA allow EPA to address environmental justice concerns. The most direct language is provided by Section 309 of the CAA, which gives EPA the authority and responsibility to review and comment in writing on certain actions proposed by other federal agencies that affect the quality of the environment. In addition, EPA's written comments must be made public at the conclusion of any review. NEPA documents that EPA reviews under Section 309 should include a statement about whether the proposed action will have an impact on minority or low-income communities. In April 1999, EPA issued its *Final Guidance for Consideration of Environmental Justice in Clean Air Act Section 309 Reviews* to provide a consistent approach to reviewing the environmental justice analyses contained in NEPA documents.

As identified by the Office of General Counsel, other actions that could be taken under the CAA include the following:[5]

- Ensuring consideration of environmental justice concerns in New Source Review (NSR) permits – NSR is a case-by-case preconstruction air permitting program under CAA for new and modified major stationary sources of criteria air pollutants. The NSR program that applies in areas designated attainment or unclassifiable for one or more National Ambient Air Quality Standard (NAAQS) air pollutants is called the Prevention of Significant Deterioration (PSD) program; the NSR program that applies in areas designated nonattainment for a NAAQS pollutant is called the nonattainment New Source Review program. Specifically, nonattainment NSR statutorily requires the consideration of an alternative analysis and an analysis of the social costs imposed by the facility's location (in a nonattainment area).[6] EPA may consider environmental justice issues under PSD review provisions pertaining to technology standards. Under CAA, EPA should issue guidance to clarify how Regions or the Environmental Appeals Board (EAB) should consider environmental justice issues in PSD/NSR permitting and review of permitting cases.

- Increasing public participation in Title V permits – Title V of the CAA requires operating permits for stationary sources of air pollutants, and prescribes public participation procedures for issuance, significant modification, and renewal of Title V permits. Specifically, under the 40 CFR Part 70/71 permitting process, EPA has authority to include measures to increase public participation in permitting actions (e.g., through guidance or rulemaking revisions).

---

[4] Richard J. Lazarus and Stephanie Tai, "Integrating Environmental Justice into EPA Permitting Authority," *Ecology Law Quarterly*, Vol. 26 (1999), pp 617 - 678.

[5] Gary Guzy memorandum.

[6] Section 173(a)(5) requires "an analysis of alternative sites, sizes, production processes and environmental control techniques for such proposed source that demonstrates that benefits of the proposed source significantly outweigh the environmental and social costs imposed as a result of its location, construction, or modification."

- Ensuring consideration of environmental justice issues in solid waste incinerator siting requirements – The CAA provides specific authority to EPA to establish siting requirements for solid waste incinerators that could include consideration of environmental justice issues. For instance, CAA Section 129(a)(3) provides that standards for new solid waste incinerators include "siting requirements that minimize, on a site specific basis, to the maximum extent practicable, potential risks to public health or the environment."

The Clean Air Act presents EPA with more opportunities to integrate environmental justice concerns into the development of substantive standards than the Agency has utilized.[7] For example, Lazarus and Tai point out that members of environmental justice communities frequently include many individuals with special sensitivities to pollution and that stricter application of EPA's statutory authority could help address some of these environmental justice concerns. They also suggest that EPA could promulgate more protective NAAQS if these special sensitivities were considered more systematically.

Recently, the EPA has initiated several pilot programs and other regulatory initiatives to promote market-oriented strategies to achieve greater pollution reduction at greater efficiencies. When designing and implementing these programs, the EPA should be particularly mindful of the potential for adverse distributional impacts that may inadvertently result if, for example, facilities trade pollution credits in a manner that may cause localized impacts. EPA should strive to design programs that continue to provide for adequate environmental review when facility emissions increase. EPA has considerable discretionary authority to impose adequate environmental justice protections in such experimental programs and should undertake to do so.

Clean Water Act (CWA)

The CWA was adopted "to restore and maintain the chemical, physical, and biological integrity of the Nation's waters." To achieve this goal, Congress prohibited the discharge from a point source of any pollutant into a water of the United States unless that discharge complies with specific requirements of the Act. Compliance is achieved by obtaining and adhering to the terms of a National Pollutant Discharge Elimination System (NPDES) permit issued by EPA or an authorized state pursuant to Section 402, or a dredge and fill permit issued by the Army Corps of Engineers or an authorized state pursuant Section 404.

Potential environmental justice issues arising under the CWA can include the following: (1) high exposure of minority or low-income subpopulations to toxicants in water due to high levels of fish consumption; (2) exposure to mixtures of chemicals in surface water due to geographical proximity of subpopulations to harmful land use practices; (3) high exposures of subpopulations to mixtures of chemicals from several media, including water; and (4) heightened sensitivity of subpopulations to toxicants present in drinking water.

EPA's Office of General Counsel has identified CWA authorities under which environmental justice issues could be addressed.[8] Examples of actions that can be taken under these authorities include the following:

- Ensuring the NPDES permits take into account environmental justice concerns – Under CWA Section 402, EPA issues NPDES permits to point sources. The permits can set discharge limitations to ensure that water quality standards are met. Water quality standards consist of designated uses of the water, which can include

---

[7] Richard J. Lazarus and Stephanie Tai.

[8] Gary Guzy memorandum.

subsistence fishing, public water supply, and recreation. In states not authorized to run the NPDES program, EPA can issue discharge permits that contain limitations appropriate to protect the specific use of subpopulations that might be particularly vulnerable (e.g., in waters where high levels of fish consumption is an "existing use").

- Increasing public participation in permitting and standard-setting process – Consistent with CWA Section 101(e), EPA can improve public participation in the permitting process (e.g., by translating notices into other languages) when it issues NPDES permits. EPA could similarly encourage states to improve public participation processes in the development of state water quality standards.

- Ensuring that state water quality standards take into account environmental justice considerations – Under the regulations at 40 CFR Section 131.12(a)(1), state water quality standards are required to provide for the protection of "existing uses" (uses actually attained in the body of water on or after November 28, 1975). The current regulations require that such uses, if actually attained, must be maintained and protected. The CWA provides EPA authority to issue guidance highlighting that high rates of fish consumption by these populations should be considered an "existing use" to be protected by state water quality standards. Similarly, EPA could issue guidance or a rule to consider subsistence fishing to be "recreation in and on water" and therefore protected by state standards.

- Ensuring consideration of environmental justice concerns in dredge and fill permits – Section 404 authorizes EPA to issue permits regulating the discharge of "dredge or fill material" to waters of the United States. Section 404 permits are issued by the Corps of Engineers and must satisfy two sets of standards: a "public interest review and Section 404(b)(1) guidelines promulgated by EPA." Environmental justice concerns could be considered during the public interest review and, under Section 404(b)(1), EPA could overturn or deny a permit citing environmental justice concerns.

Resource Conservation and Recovery Act (RCRA)

RCRA provides EPA the authority to regulate the generation, transportation, treatment, storage and disposal of hazardous wastes and the management and disposal of solid waste. EPA's Office of General Counsel has identified RCRA authorities under which environmental justice issues could be addressed.[9] Examples of actions that can be taken under these authorities include the following:

- Denying or modifying a permit based on "unacceptable risk" to certain populations – RCRA Section 3005(c)(3) provides that "each permit issued under this section shall contain such terms and conditions as the Administrator (or the State) determines necessary to protect human health and the environment." EPA has interpreted this provision to authorize the denial of a permit to a facility if it is determined that operation of the facility would pose an unacceptable risk to human health and the environment and that there are no additional permit terms or conditions that would address such a risk.

- Requiring data collection that may support environmental justice analyses – RCRA Section 3013 provides that if the Administrator determines that " the presence of any hazardous waste at a facility or site at which hazardous waste is, or has been, stored, treated, or disposed of, or the release of any such waste from such facility or site may present a substantial hazard to human health or the environment," the Administrator

---

[9] Gary Guzy memorandum.

may order a facility owner or operator to conduct reasonable monitoring, testing, analysis, and reporting to ascertain the nature and extent of such a hazard. In appropriate circumstances, EPA could use the authority to compel a facility owner or operator to carry out necessary studies, so that, pursuant to the broad authority under Section 3005(c)(3) above, EPA can establish permit terms or conditions necessary to protect human health and the environment in nearby affected communities.

- Establishing cleanup priorities based on environmental justice issues – RCRA Section 3005(e) provides EPA authority to consider environmental justice issues (such as the community-specific concerns identified above) in establishing priorities for facilities engaged in cleaning up contaminated areas under the RCRA corrective action program, RCRA Sections 3004(u), 3004(v) and 3008(h).

- Expanding public participation to consider environmental justice concerns – RCRA authorizes EPA to explore whether the RCRA permit public participation process could be expanded (e.g., consistent with the RCRA Expanded Public Participation Rule, 60 *FR* 63417) to address environmental justice concerns.

- Establishing location standards for a permit – RCRA Section 3004(o)(7) provides EPA authority to issue location standards as necessary to protect human health and the environment. Using this authority, EPA could, for example, establish minimum buffer zones between hazardous waste management facilities and sensitive areas. Facilities seeking permits would need to comply with these requirements to receive a permit.

- Amending state-issued permits – Where a state-issued permit process does not adequately address sensitive populations or other factors in violation of the authorized state program, EPA could comment on the state's proposed permit pursuant to 40 CFR 271.19 and seek to enforce the requirements as necessary to protect human health and the environment under RCRA Section 3005.

Safe Drinking Water Act (SDWA)

The SDWA regulates underground injection wells by giving EPA the authority to issue permits and rules regulating the use of such wells. As identified by EPA's Office of General Counsel, SDWA authorities could be used to address environmental justice issues through the following actions:[10]

- Denying a permit or establishing permit limits – EPA can deny a permit or establish permit limits where underground injection wells may "endanger" public health. "Endangerment" is defined to include any injection that may result in the presence of a contaminant in a drinking water supply that "may...adversely affect the health of persons." As result, where there is an injection activity that poses a special health risk to minority or low-income populations, EPA could establish special permit requirements to address the health risks, or deny the permit if the risks cannot otherwise be eliminated.

- Revising regulations – In the revisions to regulations governing "Class V" injection wells, EPA could use SDWA authority to take into account environmental justice issues such as cumulative risk and sensitive populations in developing standards necessary to prevent "endangerment." Under SDWA, EPA could also revise its regulatory requirements for siting Class 1 (hazardous waste) wells to address cumulative risk and other risk-related environmental justice issues.

---

[10] Gary Guzy memorandum.

Toxic Substances Control Act (TSCA)

TSCA includes an explicit environmental justice program, although Lazarus and Tai conclude that it is limited in scope.[11] The program refers to technical and grant assistance to the states for radon programs that target homes of low-income persons. TSCA instructs EPA to consider cumulative or synergistic effects in determining reasonable and unreasonable risks to health and the environment. Lazarus and Tai point out that these are precisely the areas that have often been overlooked in considering risks to environmental justice communities. In addition, TSCA explicitly instructs the Administrator to carry out the law by considering the environmental, economic, and social impact of any action taken.

Federal Insecticide, Fungicide, and Rodenticide Act (FIFRA)

FIFRA provides EPA with substantial authority to eliminate unreasonable risks to farm workers and others through pesticide use restrictions, disposal restrictions, labeling requirements, registration denials, and conditional registrations.[12] Again, the authority is broadly worded and open to an interpretation that promotes environmental justice concerns.

2.2   The Need for Environmental Justice Statutory Authorities

This section outlines the need for specific statutory authorities to address environmental justice. During the December NEJAC meeting, it was pointed out that the Guzy memorandum notes that while use of permitting statutes may be legally permissible, it may not always be *practical or feasible*. Furthermore, reviewing bodies have afforded substantial deference to permitting officials when they opted not to use their discretionary authority to address environmental justice concerns. For example, although the Environmental Appeals Board has noted that discretion should be exercised to further the goals of the EO to the extent practicable, it nonetheless has consistently affirmed the ultimate decision of the permitting authority in cases involving environmental justice challenges by impacted communities. Thus, the question is raised as to whether the existing statutory authorities are sufficient for addressing environmental justice concerns.

In a more general vein, Ms. Barbara Arnwine of the Lawyer's Committee for Civil Rights under Law specifically addressed the difficulties involved in advancing environmental justice though litigation. She noted that federal agencies have only infrequently pursued, and the federal courts have not been very receptive to, environmental justice cases. She viewed this in stark contrast to other areas where federal agencies are aggressive in suing to enforce federal law, such as in the antitrust and securities areas. Therefore, environmental justice communities have had to undertake litigation themselves, trying to seize opportunities to use existing laws to develop new case law and legal theories that specifically address environmental justice. However, this approach has met with only limited success in federal courts, which are often unreceptive to newly-stated legal theories, even when those theories are founded in existing laws.

Ms. Arnwine discussed 14 legal cases in which environmental justice communities had been the plaintiffs in the past two years. Of the 14 cases, 12 were unsuccessful. The 12 unsuccessful cases were argued using a variety of existing statutes and theories. Three of the 12 cases tried to use the EO to enforce the environmental justice communities' rights; another six cases used the National Environmental Policy Act and the EO; one used the Clean Air Act and the EO; and two focused on constitutional challenges and authorities under the Comprehensive Environmental Response, Compensation, and Liability Act (CERCLA, or Superfund).

---

[11] Lazarus and Tai.

[12] Ibid.

In addition, more than 70 cases involving environmental justice issues have been settled out of court – privately or administratively – over the past ten years. While the settlements may result in a "win" for the plaintiffs (e.g., an incinerator may ultimately not be built upwind from a town whose citizens are mostly poor and minority), the cases do not contribute to the body of case law or legal theories that might strengthen future plaintiffs' arguments.

In discussing some of the reasons for the outcomes of these cases, Ms. Arnwine reported that environmental justice communities typically do not have the financial means to pursue environmental justice cases as vigorously as they might. The practice of environmental justice law at the grassroots level has become "constricted," with fewer organizations currently performing such work than had been doing it eight years ago. Therefore, there are few legal experts focusing on this field, which results in fewer opportunities to pursue redress and therefore to contribute to the body of legal cases and theories to support environmental justice litigation.

Arguments used in cases against specific federal agencies that are required to comply with EO 12898 have not been very successful.[13] Indeed, the courts often defer to the outcomes of any agency's decision-making process, even if that process appears to ignore or violate environmental justice concerns. For example, the federal courts have found against plaintiffs who have tried to argue that an agency's actions were "arbitrary and capricious" when they failed to consider environmental justice issues, in violation of the Administrative Procedures Act, NEPA, and other similar laws. In addition, plaintiffs have often tried to convince the Court that an agency has failed to consider appropriate alternatives (as required under NEPA) or to assess whether a project will result in a population becoming disproportionately burdened by the project.

Simply stated, the courts do not usually second-guess federal agency decisions. This bodes badly for the many instances where agencies decline to use their discretionary authority to respond to environmental justice concerns. For example, the courts have consistently found against plaintiffs who try to use the "arbitrary" argument, stating in one case[14] that "petitioner's criticisms...involve areas in which EPA's expertise in heavily implicated, and we may not substitute our judgement for that of the Administrator." In another case,[15] the court decided that if the decision was "based on a consideration of the relevant factors" and there is no "clear error of judgment," the decision is neither arbitrary nor capricious. These decisions effectively reduce the ability of plaintiffs to criticize the decision-making process that agencies go through, as well as the decisions that result from that process. Another example can be seen with the argument that agencies do not adequately consider alternatives. In a recent decision[16] the court stated that the government did not need to consider an alternative scenario that had been proposed by the plaintiff because it was not a reasonable alternative and would not bring about the government's desired objective of efficiency. These decisions, among other similar ones, have served to limit the ability of plaintiffs to argue that an agency did not go far enough in its consideration of all possible effects of a proposed action, including environmental justice effects.

Civil rights law was once considered to be a potentially effective mechanism for securing environmental justice for individuals and communities. However, the ability to use Civil Rights law for redress against any recipient of federal funds (usually state and local agencies) appears to have been

---

[13] These conclusions are based on a detailed review of the cases that Ms. Arnwine cited in her presentation to the NEJAC. Information about the cases came from Lexis-Nexis and Cornell University's legal research site on the Internet (http://www.findlaw.com/).

[14] *Sur Contra la Contaminacion v. Environmental Protection Agency and AES Puerto Rico.* United States Court of Appeals for the First Circuit, No. 99-1855.

[15] *Morongo Band of Mission Indians vs. FAA.*

[16] *Donald Young vs. General Services Administration.*

significantly weakened by a recent Supreme Court decision. Ms. Arnwine spoke of the *Alexander vs. Sandoval*[17] case that was currently being reviewed when she made her presentation. She stated that when it is finalized, "(This) decision…will have a major impact on Title VI, its broad reach and scope…"

The *Sandoval* decision does indeed have an impact, but not a positive one from the perspective of potential plaintiffs on environmental justice cases. The decision, announced April 24, 2001, clearly limits the ability of plaintiffs to use Title VI of the Civil Rights Act as a legal basis for redress against "discrimination" or "disparate impact." In *Sandoval*, the Supreme Court affirmed its view that Section 601[18] of Title VI prohibits only <u>intentional discrimination</u>; therefore, a person may sue an agency or program only if it engages in intentional discrimination.

The Supreme Court then went on to analyze Section 602 of Title VI, which was the basis for the *Sandoval* lawsuit. The Court assumed for purposes of litigation that Section 602 permits federal agencies to pass regulations that prohibit discriminatory effects in the conduct of their programs. <u>Title VI does not allow individuals to go to court to enforce these adverse impact regulations</u>. Thus, there is no private right of action to enforce the disparate impact regulations promulgated by agencies under Section 602.[19] In the Court's view, an individual seeking redress for this type of discrimination is limited to filing a complaint with the offending agency.

Plaintiffs have had limited success promoting environmental justice by using housing law and specific Constitutional issues, particularly those related to the 14th Amendment. As Ms. Arnwine states, "…the courts listen harder when there is a Constitutional challenge." The most successful environmental justice cases have used historic segregation patterns to argue that certain decisions which exacerbate environmental inequities serve to perpetuate these preexisting segregations in violation of the Equal Protection clause of the Constitution, Title VI (of the Civil Rights Act), and the Fair Housing Act. However, many environmental justice cases have no link to fair housing issues or to fundamental Constitutional questions, so this avenue is limited in its applicability.

Despite the paucity of cases that specifically cast their claims in terms of "environmental justice", many cases involving environmental justice communities have been successfully prosecuted as criminal actions. The Department of Justice, for example, has successfully prosecuted defendants in cases in which pollution has impacted communities covered by EO 12898. These cases include successful convictions of defendants who illegally applied commercial pesticides, designed for outdoor use, in low-income homes around the country; those who exploited homeless workers by making them participate in illegal asbestos removals without proper safety precautions or training; and those who illegally dumped hazardous wastes in low-income and minority neighborhoods.[20] These cases have been brought using existing enforcement tools – such as OSHA requirements for training for asbestos mitigation and RCRA requirements for waste disposal – that apply even in the absence of environmental justice requirements.

---

[17] *Alexander, Director, Alabama Dept. of Public Safety, et al. v. Sandoval, individually and on behalf of all others similarly situated.* No. 99-1908. Argued January 16, 2001. Decided April 24, 2001.

[18] Under Section 601, no person can be discriminatorily denied the benefits of any program or activity that receives federal funds.

[19] As noted by the dissent, disparate impact regulations might be enforceable in court as as supporting a violation of Section 1983 of the Civil Rights Act, a provision that does allow a private right of action. The issue is presently pending in a recent case.

[20] Sylvia Liu, "Environmental Justice: An Overview of Legal Issues," United States Attorneys' Bulletin, U.S. Department of Justice, February 2000, pp. 1-6.

However, the Department of Justice pays particular attention to and pursues criminal cases that have environmental justice implications.[21]

In summary, there appears to be little case law and few legal theories that have succeeded in using the EO 12898 to challenge agency actions. The primary obstacle appears to be the strong deference afforded to agencies, such as EPA's implementation of environmental laws. With respect to the Civil Rights laws, the *Sandoval* decision has curtailed the ability to prosecute disparate impacts in court proceedings, although there have been a few successful cases involving the Fair Housing Act. Constitutional arguments, such as those based upon violations of the equal protection clause, have been uniformly unsuccessful due to the requirement to provide sufficient evidence of discriminatory intent. Given these limitations, legislation that amends the federal civil rights laws to specifically provide for a private right of action to address disparate impacts, or legislation explicitly addressing environmental justice, may be necessary to better address environmental justice concerns.

3. PROGRESS IN FEDERAL AGENCY IMPLEMENTATION

This section presents findings on progress that federal agencies have made in integrating environmental justice issues into their programs and policies. At the December 2000 NEJAC meeting, representatives from a number of federal agencies made presentations that provided insight into the progress that their agencies have made in integrating environmental justice into agency policies, programs, and activities, as required under the Executive Order. Given that the presentations by agency officials were necessarily brief, this report supplements the presentations with information derived from additional sources, such as government agency websites, reports, and a recent article in the Environmental Law Institute's *Environmental Law Reporter* (hereafter "ELI article").[22] It must be noted, however, that all sources of information about federal agency implementation of the environmental justice EO rely upon accurate representations made by agency personnel; none of the information has been independently verified.

The presentations made at the December 2000 meeting did not follow a consistent format for content and topics to be covered. Therefore, in order to analyze the information on progress being made in this document, the information presented was put into a consistent framework. Section 3.1 below describes the functional framework used for this report, which consists of four programmatic components. Section 3.2 summarizes the information presented on each federal agency, re-organized according to the functional framework. Where additional details were available from other sources, these are noted. Section 3.3 uses the data in Section 3.2 to provide an overall evaluation of federal agency progress in implementing environmental justice.

3.1 Introduction to Functional Framework

The functional framework consists of four broad categories of agency activities or actions. These broad categories are intended to capture the universe of agency activities or actions as they relate to implementing the environmental justice principles set forth in EO 12898.

---

[21] "For the purposes of the Justice Department, an environmental justice matter is any civil or criminal matter where the conduct or action at issue may involve a disproportionate and adverse environmental or human health effect on an identifiable low-income or minority community or federally-recognized tribe." Attorneys are directed to "be alert to factors indicating a possible environmental justice matter as a case develops." Department of Justice, Guidance Concerning Environmental Justice. http://www.usdoj.gov/archive/enrd/ejguide.html.

[22] Denis Binder et. al., "A Survey of federal Agency Responses to President Clinton's Executive Order 12898 on Environmental Justice," 31 *Environmental Law Reporter* 11,133 (2001). The information in this ELI article was based in part upon agencies responses to a survey submitted to the agencies by the authors of the article, and as noted in the article, the information was not independently verified.

- *Policies and evaluation.* These include manifestations of support from senior agency officials for integrating environmental justice into agency operations. Evidence of such support includes policies, operational strategies and planning documents, and evaluation of internal procedure implementation.

- *Organizational investments.* These are internal investments that an agency has made to implement its environmental justice programs, such as new staff positions, new offices, training, or specific discrete programs.

- *Programmatic procedures.* These include mechanisms by which agencies have incorporated environmental justice issues into their ongoing operations. These could include, for example, an internal assessment of whether and to what extent the agency's operations have an effect on the environment. These effects may have positive or negative consequences to an environmental justice community. Programmatic procedures could also include means to address environmental justice in day-to-day operations and programs. One example is specific guidance on how to incorporate environmental justice into the NEPA process.

- *External outreach.* External outreach comprises those activities that are focused on reaching out to potentially affected populations and communities, such as providing technical assistance, financial assistance, training, and opportunities for public participation in decision-making.

This functional framework provides a lens for agencies to use to examine their activities and to better assess what they are doing to their individual strategies to promote environmental justice principles. It further provides a framework that agencies may use to organize future presentations describing their environmental justice accomplishments and activities.

3.2   Presentation of Federal Agency Programs

The sections below present information on environmental justice activities in each federal agency represented at the December 2000 NEJAC meeting, consistent with the functional framework described above.

3.2.1   Department of Justice

This section presents environmental justice activities and initiatives within the Department of Justice (DOJ), as presented by Ms. Lois Schiffer, Assistant Attorney General, at the December 2000 NEJAC meeting, and from additional sources that provided explanatory details about DOJ's environmental justice activities.

Policies and Evaluations

Ms. Schiffer stated that DOJ's approach is to implement the principles of the Executive Order No. 12898 on Environmental Justice in all of the Department's litigation. A review of supporting documentation and websites indicates that DOJ issued a Department-wide Environmental Justice Strategy in 1995 to implement these principles.[23] In addition, DOJ has also issued the *Department of*

---

[23] The U.S. DOJ Environmental Justice Strategy (1995) is referenced in the Department of Justice Guidance Concerning Environmental Justice (available at www.usdoj.gov/archive/enrd/ejguide.html) and also referenced in Binder, et al., *supra.* The U.S. DOJ Environmental Justice Strategy is no longer

Justice Guidance Concerning Environmental Justice, which includes Department goals and suggestions for implementation.[24] This Guidance contains no prescriptive elements of Department policy; rather, it provides a set of guidelines and suggestions for how DOJ attorneys can incorporate environmental justice principles into their work.

Ms. Schiffer stated that DOJ has also, as a matter of Department policy, focused upon two specific areas: 1) enforcing provisions of the Residential Lead-Based Paint Reduction Act, and 2) enforcing cleanups of Superfund sites contaminated with hazardous wastes. The Department also assists with redevelopment of brownfield sites.[25]

Organizational Investments

In her presentation, Ms. Schiffer did not specifically address DOJ organizational investments supporting environmental justice. Other sources, however, provide an indication of DOJ's efforts in this area. According to the ELI article, DOJ provides training on environmental justice issues to new hires, and each litigating section was provided with environmental justice training after the Executive Order No. 12898 on Environmental Justice was signed. In addition, environmental justice concepts are now incorporated into DOJ internal manuals and training materials. For example, the *U.S. Attorney's Training Manual on Civil Rights* includes references to environmental justice.[26]

The ELI article also indicates that DOJ has two work groups that help promote environmental justice principles and goals within the Department. The Working Group on Environmental Justice monitors environmental justice efforts across the Department. The Working Group on Environmental Health Risks to Children has focused on reducing environmental risks in communities. Ultimately, however, much of the legal implementation of environmental justice principles is left to the discretion of individual DOJ attorneys assigned to specific cases.

Programmatic Procedures

In her presentation, Ms. Schiffer did not discuss specific DOJ programmatic procedures supporting environmental justice. Other sources, however, provide an indication of DOJ's efforts in this area. A review of the DOJ website indicated that several programs have included environmental justice components as part of their guidance for conducting environmental assessments and environmental impact statements under the National Environmental Policy Act (NEPA).[27]

External Outreach

---

available directly on the DOJ website. To obtain a copy of this document it is necessary to contact the FOIA conventional reading room at DOJ. See http://www.usdoj.gov/enrd/foia.htm for the address and phone number. Note that it is not necessary to submit a FOIA request to obtain the document.

[24] Department of Justice Guidance Concerning Environmental Justice is available at: www.usdoj.gov/archive/enrd/ejguide.html).

[25] It is unclear at this time whether the new administration will continue the policy of the previous administration in these areas. DOJ is currently undertaking a reorganization and review of Department priorities as a normal element of transition between administrations and in response to the events of September 11, 2001.

[26] Binder, et al.

[27] See http://www.ojp.usdoj.gov/cpo/eaoutln.pdf for an example of guidance on preparing an EA, and see http://www.ojp.usdoj.gov/cpo/eissow.pdf for an example of guidance on preparing an EIS.

In her presentation, Ms. Schiffer stated that DOJ strives to provide for meaningful community participation in Department decision-making. She cites examples involving settlement of affirmative civil enforcement cases under the CAA and under the Residential Lead-Based Paint Hazard Reduction Act. In one instance, DOJ settled litigation with the City of Chicago over complaints related to the CAA. Under the terms of the settlement, the City agreed to pay a fine and perform supplemental environmental projects (SEPs) valued at $700,000. She reported that the SEPs were selected with significant community input. In litigation against landlords who had not notified tenants about possible lead hazards in their properties, DOJ, with input from the community, was able to get the real estate companies to undertake lead abatement activities to remedy the problems and to buy portable devices to test blood lead levels in children.

A second example of external outreach cited by Ms. Schiffer is DOJ's community-based programs. She specifically mentioned DOJ's "Operation Weed and Seed", which focuses Department and community resources on "weeding" out crime, drugs, and gang activity and "seeding" human services and neighborhood revitalization. Ms. Schiffer indicated that four "Weed and Seed" sites (out of a total of approximately 250 sites) had been selected as case studies that will be examined to identify and understand community environmental issues, and to develop a strategy to address the problems. According to one source, these sites have made environmental protection part of their community revitalization strategy; this strategy encompasses brownfields restoration, targeted enforcement against illegal hazardous waste operations, establishment of citizen hotlines, and a lead hazard remediation program.[28]

Another example of external outreach from a community-based program presented by Ms. Schiffer is the Community Oriented Policing Services (COPS). According to Ms. Schiffer, this effort was in its beginning stages in December 2000. DOJ had been working with EPA and the Department of Interior to incorporate environmental protection into the community policing model. DOJ was also making funding available through the COPS program to pay for environmental officers. In FY 2000 this effort was primarily directed to Indian tribes.

3.2.2 Department of Defense

Ms. Sherri Goodman (Deputy Under Secretary of Defense for Environmental Security) presented the status of Department of Defense (DoD) efforts to implement EO 12898.

Policies and Evaluation

In her presentation, Ms. Goodman indicated that DoD has an overall strategy for implementing EO 12898 that is focused on institutional change rather than one-time events. The strategy includes five major principles: promotion of partnerships with all stakeholders; identifying impacts of DoD activities on environmental justice communities; streamlining government; improving day-to-day operations at installations related to environmental justice concerns; and fostering non-discrimination in all DoD programs and activities.

Ms. Goodman indicated several ways in which DoD has developed overall policies that direct the operations to consider environmental justice issues. First, she indicated that DoD has integrated environmental justice analysis into its NEPA process. Specifically, a requirement to analyze the impacts of a proposed action and alternatives on populations covered by EO 12898 was included in DoD Instruction 4715.9 *Environmental Planning and Analysis* (May 1996). She also indicated that each of the military departments has also incorporated environmental justice analysis into its respective NEPA and environmental planning instructions and regulations. For example, the Air Force includes environmental justice analysis in Air Force Instruction 32-7061, *The Environmental Impact Analysis Process* and has

---

[28] Ibid.

issued *a Guide for Environmental Justice Analysis with the Environmental Impact Analysis Process* (November 1997).

As another example, Ms. Goodman stated that DoD issued its American Indian and Alaska Native Policy in October 1998. The policy which was signed by the Secretary of Defense, allows tribes a significant role in decision-making on cleanup issues and defines government-to-government coordination. Ms. Goodman stated that this represents a major effort by senior leadership to advance Native American environmental justice considerations within the Department's business practices.

Organizational Investments

With respect to organizational investments, Ms. Goodman mentioned that DoD has produced a training video for military and civilian personnel. It explains the requirements of EO 12898 and how it impacts DoD policies and programs. The goal of the video is to help increase awareness of environmental justice issues and infuse the spirit and intent of the Executive Order No. 12898 on Environmental Justice into decision-making processes. In addition, DoD has developed a sensitivity training program on American Indian and Alaskan Native cultures for personnel at all levels who may need to work with tribes. The training covers the DoD American Indian and Alaska Native Policy and educates personnel in how to interact with tribes on a government-to-government basis.

Programmatic Procedures

Ms. Goodman reported that DoD has used cooperative agreements with tribes to assist them in working directly with DoD to address environmental impacts on tribal lands. At least 15 cooperative agreements or memoranda of understanding have been signed with federally recognized tribes or coalitions of tribes. The cooperative agreements allow tribes to receive technical assistance and training and allow tribes to participate in and undertake environmental cleanup and mitigation actions. Ms. Goodman reported that this has enabled tribes to play a significant role in the decisions and actions that affect their communities.

External Outreach

Ms. Goodman reported that DoD conducts a major outreach effort through its Restoration Advisory Boards (RABs). RABs provide communities affected by DoD cleanup activities with an opportunity to participate in environmental restoration decisions. RABs are intended to represent all sectors of the local community and be inclusive of diverse citizen groups. To improve RAB members' understanding of environmental restoration issues, DoD established its Technical Assistance for Public Participation (TAPP) grant program that provides funding for independent technical advice and consultation to community groups. RABs are designed to allow community members to play an active role in cleanup decisions that impact their communities. Ms. Goodman stated that there are more than 250 RABs nationwide and that most of them have been very successful.

DoD also conducts public outreach efforts to solicit comment and opinion from environmental justice communities. Ms. Goodman mentioned the example of the Stakeholder Forum, held in St. Louis, which brought together representatives of environmental justice communities and interested parties to discuss environmental justice issues with Ms. Goodman and her staff.

Ms. Goodman stated that DoD has an environmental justice website with access to guidance documents and environmental justice information. DoD also reportedly translates documents into languages other than English and places notices of meetings in community newspapers. Many DoD installations also have active public outreach programs to engage the local community, but it is unclear how many of these include a strong environmental justice focus.

3.2.3 Department of Energy

This section identifies the actions taken by the U.S. Department of Energy (DOE) to incorporate environmental justice principles into the Department's framework, in accordance with EO12898. At the December NEJAC meeting, several speakers updated the Council on DOE's progress:

- Dr. Carolyn Huntoon, Assistant Secretary for Environmental Management, offered the Executive Council a description of DOE successes in weaving environmental justice into the Department's fabric.

- Ms. Heather Stockwell, Director of Science, Office of Health Studies, presented and briefly discussed a handout that summarized the public health activities that are conducted at DOE sites. The handout was distributed to members of the Health and Research Subcommittee.

- Derrick Watchman, Director of Indian Affairs, explained to the Indigenous Peoples Subcommittee how DOE has addressed energy-related problems that have harmed the living environments of tribes and Alaskan Natives.

Policies and Evaluation

According to Dr. Huntoon, environmental justice has become an integral part of DOE's policies, programs, and culture. Although Dr. Huntoon did not provide specifics on this integration, the DOE website indicates that in 1995 DOE developed a formal strategy for promoting environmental justice principles within its operations.[29] The strategy presents four goals: (1) identify and address programs, policies, and activities that have a disproportionately high adverse human health and environmental affects on minority or low-income populations; (2) ensure that public participation becomes a fundamental component of all program operations, activities, and decisions; (3) improve research and data collection practices of departmental Headquarters and Field Offices; and (4) enhance departmental leadership by integrating environmental justice criteria.

Organizational Investments

Dr. Huntoon described several organizational investments. First, DOE has appointed an environmental justice coordinator for its Office of Economic Impact and Diversity, and has designated points of contact for environmental justice issues in each of its major programs and field centers. Second, DOE is offering environmental justice training to educate and sensitize managers and staff. To address environmental justice concerns in Indian country, DOE has established a tribal liaison, a position designed to facilitate communication between the Department and tribal leaders. The DOE website also indicates that DOE has created a Steering Committee to ensure that the agency's strategy for implementing environmental justice is executed.[30] The Committee includes four Secretarial Officers and a department-wide Working Group that is represented by a member of each Headquarters and Field Component.

Programmatic Procedures

Although they were not explicitly addressed in Dr. Huntoon's presentation, DOE has established procedures for incorporating environmental justice concerns into day-to-day operations that have

---

[29] "U.S. Department of Energy Environmental Justice Strategy, Executive Order No. 12898 on Environmental Justice 12898, April 1995." http://www.em.doe.gov/stake/envjus.html.

[30] Ibid.

environmental impacts. In particular, DOE has assessed how environmental justice considerations can be integrated into the response and cleanup actions authorized by the Comprehensive Environmental Response, Compensation, and Liability Act (CERCLA).[31] For example, DOE has called for more in-depth site assessments to determine whether low-income or minority communities are potential receptors of contamination, or are at risk due to patterns of consumption that lead to increased exposures to environmental hazards.[32] On the issue of resource allocation, Dr. Huntoon reported that DOE has also incorporated environmental justice criteria into its review process for funding grantees, as well as in the NEPA review process.

In other presentations, DOE representatives described how DOE has incorporated environmental justice concerns into existing programs. According to Ms. Stockwell, DOE has developed an agenda to conduct public health activities to address contamination at 12 major sites across the country. DOE developed this agenda in conjunction with several federal departments, such as the Agency for Toxic Substances and Disease Registry, Centers for Disease Control and Prevention, the National Center for Environmental Health, and the National Institute for Occupational Safety and Health. In his presentation to the Indigenous Peoples Subcommittee, Mr. Watchman described ways in which DOE has supported Native American tribes in overcoming the "electrical divide" that has occurred in their communities. DOE has brought needed energy resources to Native Americans by providing electricity produced by federal generating facilities and by developing renewable resources of energy. Since tribal and Native Alaskan lands are often remote, the development of renewable forms of energy has become a top priority for the Department.

External Outreach

Dr. Huntoon told the Executive Committee that DOE has committed itself to helping minority populations remedy environmental problems in their respective neighborhoods. Perhaps at the forefront of this commitment is the Environmental Justice Resource Center, a DOE-sponsored center located at Clark Atlanta University. The center operates as a resource, policy, and informational clearinghouse for issues concerning environmental justice, race, land use, and equality.

DOE has also furthered its partnership with People of Color and Disenfranchised Communities Environmental Health Network (the Coalition) by helping with their "Implementation Plan," which outlines activities to cultivate positive relationships between community members and agency officials and to address problems within impacted communities.[33] After teaming up with the National Conference of Black Mayors, DOE has offered assistance to disadvantaged communities for improving sewage systems, waste incineration facilities, and other sources of environmental concerns. Specific DOE projects include the following:

- Spanish Translation Project -- DOE has translated many documents concerning environmental justice into Spanish, including EO 12898, an accompanying presidential memorandum, and a technical assistance document.[34] DOE also operates a bilingual website on "green building" and other environmental issues.

- Savannah River -- DOE's Office of Environmental Management has partnered with EPA's Office of Federal Facilities Restoration, Savannah State University, and Citizens

---

[31] "Incorporating Environmental Justice Principles into the CERCLA Process." DOE, Office of Minority Impact, May 1998.

[32] Ibid.

[33] http://www.em.doe.gov/public/envjust/people.html.

[34] Ibid.

for Environmental Justice to assist Savannah River communities that are located near a DOE facility that has had negative impacts on their environment, reported Dr. Huntoon. Through workshops and community activities—including literature exhibits on environmental radiation and weekly radio programs—DOE has attempted to inform residents on how to protect their communities.

- Americorps "Salmoncorps" Project -- DOE trained more than 70 participants from five Native American tribes in environmental restoration techniques to repair the vital salmon habitat in the Columbia River Basin in Washington, Oregon, and Idaho.[35]

3.2.4   Department of Transportation

This section presents environmental justice activities and initiatives within the Department of Transportation (DOT), as presented by Mr. Ron Stroman at the December 2000 NEJAC meeting, and from additional sources that provided explanatory details about DOT's environmental justice activities.

Policies and Evaluations

Most of the work of the Department of Transportation involves setting policies and procedures to be followed by state and local governments in planning and constructing transportation facilities that receive federal funding or support. DOT requires an extensive planning process by both states and metropolitan areas to identify potential projects and move them forward to actual construction. Mr. Stroman stated that DOT has focused environmental justice efforts at the front end of the planning process for new facilities, be they roads, rail, airports, or other facilities. In October 1999, the Federal Highway Administration (FHWA) and the Federal Transit Administration (FTA) issued a memorandum that clarified how environmental justice should be considered as part of the overall statewide and metropolitan planning process. As of December 2000, FHWA and FTA were in the process of issuing a final rule on the planning process, which includes requirements for considering the potential environmental justice impacts of proposed facilities.[36]

According to the ELI article, DOT Order 5610.2 was issued in April 1997 and makes environmental justice considerations part of the Department's official Title VI policy.[37] The Order describes how the Department will integrate environmental justice into daily operations. FHWA issued a parallel environmental justice Order 6640.23 on December 2, 1998.

Organizational Investments

According to Mr. Stroman, DOT has created an Environmental Justice Review Committee comprising senior DOT officials. This committee reviews the potential impacts of transportation projects on minority communities. Mr. Stroman stated that DOT has also conducted a number of workshops and training on environmental justice issues for Department personnel and state and local planning organizations. For example, the ELI article reports that FHWA's Office of Civil Rights had developed an anti-discrimination training course that includes an environmental justice module.[38]

Programmatic Procedures

---

[35] Ibid.

[36] Ron Stroman presentation before the National Environmental Justice Advisory Council, December 11, 2000. Volume 1.

[37] Binder, et al.

[38] Ibid.

The joint planning rule and the October 1999 memorandum discussed above are applied to the metropolitan planning organization (MPO) planning certification process. This certification process enables state and local governments to maintain eligibility for receiving federal transportation funds. DOT can choose to not certify, issue conditional certifications, or certify that MPOs meet DOT requirements for planning processes. Thus far, DOT has issued two conditional certifications that essentially require the MPOs to show how they plan to incorporate environmental justice principles into their planning process before DOT will issue a full certification.

The ELI article also reports that DOT established an environmental justice data bank to collect, maintain, and analyze information on the race, color, national origin, and income level of persons adversely affected by DOT activities. In addition, DOT's Order 5610.2 requires certain procedures to be followed in the NEPA process to ensure consideration of environmental justice principles.[39]

External Outreach

DOT guidelines require stakeholder involvement during the planning process, which is typically done by state and local agencies responsible for the process. Mr. Stroman indicated that DOT's outreach efforts occur through its oversight and review function and in selected cases where environmental justice lawsuits have been filed by local organizations. For example, DOT reportedly has been a key player in the environmental justice review underway in Atlanta. DOT also settled an environmental justice lawsuit involving Jersey Heights, Maryland.

3.2.5 Department of Interior

This section presents the progress being made within the U.S. Department of the Interior (DOI), as presented by Mr. Willie Taylor and Ms. Lisa Guide at the December NEJAC meeting, and from additional sources that provided explanatory details about DOI's environmental justice activities.

Policies and Evaluations

According to Mr. Taylor, DOI has developed an *Environmental Justice Strategic Plan*, which is available on the Department's website.[40] This plan contains two main components: natural and coastal resources, and relationships with people. According to the website, DOI's strategy dates from 1995, and outlines the following four goals:

- Involve minority and low-income communities in environmental decisions and assure public access to DOI environmental information.

- Provide DOI employees with environmental justice guidance and, with the help of minority and low-income communities, develop training that will reduce their exposure to environmental health and safety hazards.

- Use and expand DOI's science, research, and data collection capabilities on innovative solutions to environmental justice-related issues.

---

[39] Ibid.

[40] Details on the strategy are located at http://www.doi.gov/oepc/ej2.html.

- Use public partnership opportunities with environmental and grassroots groups, business, academic, labor organizations, and federal, tribal, and local governments to advance environmental justice.

DOI has a decentralized structure, and each of its eight bureaus uses its own guidance or other documentation to implement the Department's strategy independently. For example, since August 1993, the Bureau of Land Management (BLM) has had a formal policy of identifying minority, tribal, or low-income populations that may be affected by a pending decision during the preliminary scoping process under NEPA; assessing the impacts on these populations; and involving these populations in the public participation process. BLM policy also emphasizes compliance with requirements under the American Indian Religious Freedom Act (AIRFA) and the National Historic Preservation Act (NHPA), which mandate public input from American Indian tribes when the Bureau's projects may affect Indian religious practices or sacred areas.[41] The Office of Surface Mining (OSM) reports that as a matter of policy, it places a high priority on incorporating meaningful public participation of low-income, minority community members and members of the Native American community in its dealings with the states, tribes, citizens and industry.[42]

Organizational Investments

Mr. Taylor reported that DOI has assigned coordinators for each DOI bureau. Each coordinator is responsible for ensuring that environmental justice is incorporated into the missions of each of the eight bureaus within the Department, as is one staff in the Solicitor's Office. Nine individuals within DOI, therefore, have environmental justice responsibilities.

The ELI article reports that primary responsibility for environmental justice oversight and initiatives at DOI rests with the Director of DOI's Office of Environmental Policy and Compliance.[43] Environmental justice is only one of the Director's responsibilities, and as such no single person at DOI is solely responsible for environmental justice compliance. Rather, as Mr. Taylor pointed out, many of its efforts are diffused throughout the Department, which is consistent with its decentralized organizational structure. Some bureaus have established offices or made other organizational investments in environmental justice. For example, BLM has established a National Native American Program Office, located in New Mexico, to coordinate policy and guidance for all BLM programs. Because of the special relationships between the United States and Indian tribes, the Bureau of Reclamation (BOR) has Native American Affairs Offices in Washington, D.C., the Regions, and many area offices. These offices are primarily concerned with making Reclamation services more readily available to tribes and making sure that Indian concerns are considered by BOR.

The ELI further reports that no centralized process identifies, tracks, or evaluates environmental justice-related matters. Each individual bureau is responsible for oversight and evaluation of environmental justice affairs within its jurisdiction. Although there may be a lack of consistency among bureaus, there is sharing of information about their respective initiatives.[44]

Programmatic Procedures

DOI has made a point of working to improve its procedures and guidance, particularly under NEPA. DOI reportedly intends to further expand opportunities for community input in the NEPA public

---

[41] http://www.doi.gov/oepc/goal1.html.

[42] Ibid.

[43] Binder, et al.

[44] Ibid.

involvement process by actively seeking the involvement of minority, low-income communities and Indian tribal governments.[45]

According to the ELI article, the individual bureaus have taken steps to incorporate environmental justice consideration in guidelines and procedures. The U.S. Fish and Wildlife Service (FWS) continually updates its guidance for subsistence taking of fish and wildlife on federal lands in Alaska. When they developed the guidance, a major effort was undertaken to consult with all Alaska Native villages, Alaska Native regional corporations, and major Alaska Native groups in Alaska. BOR implemented procedures attempting to ensure that its projects do not adversely impact Indian trust assets. The National Park Service (NPS) is revising its NEPA guidelines to include guidance on environmental justice issues. The Office of Surface Mining (OSM) has established an Advisory Committee under the Federal Advisory Committee Act (FACA) to advise it on specific regulatory issues. This committee will be comprised of members from the States, tribes, industry, and residents of coalfield regions (coal is a major focus of OSM), many of whom are low-income.[46]

External Outreach

Although Mr. Taylor did not discuss DOI's external outreach efforts in detail, the ELI article reports that DOI's stated goals are to involve minority and low-income communities in the environmental decision-making process and to assure public access to their environmental information.[47] As stated on the DOI web site, DOI also seeks to use public partnership opportunities with environmental and grassroots groups, business, academic, labor organizations, and federal, tribal, and local governments to advance environmental justice.[48]

Following Mr. Taylor's presentation, Ms. Guide provided a representative example of DOI's efforts using public partnerships. DOI has engaged in a campaign to educate the public about persistent organic pollutants (POPs) in Alaska and their impact, such as working with EPA and NOAA to produce a report called "Contaminants in Alaska."

More detailed information about DOI's activities on environmental justice are available on the Department's website.[49] Some examples include the following:

- Fish and Wildlife Service (FWS) -- FWS has several successful programs that target inner city and other indigent groups. One such project is the establishment of Job Corps centers, located on three refuges, which provide training on conservation activities. The Partners for Cultural Diversity Program focuses on encouraging minorities to pursue natural resource careers. The Resource Apprenticeships Program (RAPS) works with the BIA, Department of Fish, Wildlife & Parks, and the USDA's Forest Service to organize work and educational experiences for minority and low-income high school and college students. In the Alaska Region, FWS conducts numerous hearings and informal meetings associated with decisions or planning processes that affect "bush" communities. FWS project leaders, planners, and biologists are expected to make contact with Alaska Native tribes, organizations/groups and other interest groups as early as possible within the process

---

[45] Ibid.

[46] Ibid.

[47] Ibid.

[48] http://www.doi.gov/oepc.

[49] Ibid.

to ensure that all affected parties understand FWS proposals. FWS also employs Alaska Native interpreters who assist in gathering data within their communities. A wide variety of fish and wildlife and environmental information and education projects are done in conjunction with Alaska Native corporations and local schools in the bush communities.

- National Park Service (NPS) -- The NPS has extensive public involvement and participation programs incorporated into its planning and decision-making process. NPS makes diligent efforts to involve potentially affected publics in scoping, development of alternatives, analysis of impacts, and public review of NPS proposed activities. These efforts have included the development of written materials for non-English speaking populations, as well as the use of translators for non-literate, non-English speaking populations. NPS also has numerous partnerships programs with youth corps and conservation organizations. In urban areas, these programs serve as a means to introduce minority and low-income children and young adults to environmental and conservation issues. In developing the General Management Plan for Chaco Culture National Historic Park as well as for the El Malpais National Monument, NPS staff had extensive involvement with Native American groups, using interpreters to facilitate interchange between NPS personnel and local Native American residents. In the Washington, D.C. area, NPS has taken steps to keep Latin-American communities involved in the NPS environmental decision-making process to address user conflicts in the area surrounding the tennis stadium at Rock Creek Park. In order to fully involve local Latin-American soccer users, NPS prepared Spanish translations of documents to explain the environmental planning process.

- Bureau of Land Management -- According to DOI's website, on Navajo lands, BLM provides multi-language signs at risk sites that alert the public, in English, Spanish, and Navajo, to the fact that hazardous materials are present at the site. In addition, BLM is considering the translation of brochures and other documentation on environmental issues that potentially impact minority and low-income populations. BLM in Oregon participates in ongoing tribal Leadership Forums hosted by the BIA to explore federal/tribal relations in the Northwest. All BLM State Offices include the tribal governments on mailing lists for news releases, scoping letters and notices, and various other correspondences.

- Bureau of Indian Affairs (BIA) -- Tribal governments and their members always contribute to BIA actions involving public participation and access to information because the majority of BIA's actions are initiated by tribes or individual Indian landowners. BIA regulations, handbooks, and guidance documents are subject to tribal scrutiny prior to approval. Tribal concerns are discussed and mentioned throughout BIA's NEPA documents, especially in the "Alternatives" and "Socio-Economic" sections.

- Office of Surface Mining -- In an effort to ensure that all members of affected communities have the opportunity to convey their ideas and concerns to the office on decisions that affect their community, OSM has established proactive public participation procedures that ensure the attendance of interpreters at all public hearings for non-English speaking participants. OSM advertises public hearings and meetings in local media other than the local newspaper, and holds public meetings and hearings in locations and facilities in the affected communities whenever possible.

- Minerals Management Service (MMS) -- The MMS produces some public information documents in Spanish, Japanese, and Alaska Native languages to ensure that non-

English speaking populations, potentially affected by OCS activities, are made aware of those activities. Examples of translated documents include press releases, "fact sheets," and layperson's summaries of technical studies and reports.

3.2.6   EPA (Region 6)

Mr. Jerry Clifford (Deputy Regional Administrator Region VI) presented the status of EPA's implementation of EO 12898. However, rather than provide details on what EPA has accomplished, he presented his vision for addressing environmental justice issues in the future. Therefore, much of the information presented below on EPA progress relies on additional research sources.

Policies and Evaluation

Mr. Clifford acknowledged the leadership in the promotion of environmental justice concerns shown by senior EPA management, including the Administrator. The EPA website indicates that in 1993, the former EPA Administrator established environmental justice as one of the seven guiding principles in the Agency's Strategic Plan. EPA also published an *Environmental Justice Strategy: Executive Order 12898* (April 1995), which contains five major focus areas: 1) Public Participation and Accountability, Partnerships, Outreach, and Communication with Stakeholders; 2) Health and Environmental Research; 3) Data Collection, Analysis, and Stakeholder Access to Public Information; 4) American Indian and Indigenous Environmental Protection; and 5) Enforcement, Compliance Assurance, and Regulatory Reviews. To supplement the Environmental Justice Strategy, EPA released its *Environmental Justice Implementation Plan* in August 1997.

Organizational Investments

Mr. Clifford mentioned that EPA established the national Office of Environmental Justice (OEJ) within its Office of Enforcement and Compliance Assurance (OECA). EPA's environmental justice website indicates that OEJ was established in 1992 to oversee the integration of environmental justice into EPA policies, programs, and activities. It also serves as the focal point for environmental justice outreach and education activities and provides technical and financial assistance to environmental justice communities. EPA serves as the lead agency of the Interagency Working Group on Environmental Justice. In addition to OEJ, EPA has an Office of Civil Rights (OCR) to address claims brought under Title VI of the Civil Rights Act and to provide a focus for Agency attention on discrimination issues.

Mr. Clifford stated that each of EPA's ten Regions also has a regional EJ program to serve as a primary focal point for environmental justice issues. According to Clifford, the main goal of these offices is to integrate environmental justice into Agency activities and guide environmental justice action within the various EPA programs. He suggested that the future direction of environmental justice should be to fully integrate environmental justice protections into EPA and other federal agency decision-making processes so that these types of offices of environmental justice or their equivalents would no longer be necessary.

Mr. Charles Lee (Associate Director of Policy and Interagency Liason, Office of Environmental Justice (OEJ), EPA) described the importance of EPA's newly developed Environmental Justice Training Collaborative (EJTC) that he believes may provide the link between the concepts of environmental justice and government policies and program development and implementation. Mr. Jack McGraw (Deputy Regional Administrator Region VIII) explained that the EJTC is an effort – supported by all ten of EPA's Regions – that aims to promote environmental justice within the Agency and raise its profile in the program offices. He stated that the goals were to provide a fundamental course on environmental justice which would be piloted with a number of stakeholders and to develop a national team of trainers (some of them non-EPA staff).

Programmatic Procedures

EPA has incorporated environmental justice analysis into its own internal NEPA review procedures (40 CFR Part 6) and issued its *Final Guidance for Incorporating Environmental Justice Concerns in EPA's NEPA Compliance Analysis* in April 1998. It should be noted, however, that many of EPA's actions are exempt from NEPA, so this guidance might have a more limited effect than it would in other federal agency contexts. In addition to its internal NEPA processes, EPA has authority to review NEPA documentation from other federal agencies under Section 309 of the Clean Air Act. EO 12898 directs EPA to use this authority to ensure that other federal agencies analyze environmental justice impacts. In April 1999, EPA issued its *Final Guidance for Consideration of Environmental Justice in Clean Air Act Section 309 Reviews* to provide a consistent approach to reviewing the environmental justice analyses contained in NEPA documents.

External Outreach

EPA's environmental justice website indicates that OEJ administers a grant program for community- and university-based organizations to increase environmental awareness, expand outreach, and provide training and education to resolve environmental problems. Another source reports that OEJ has awarded over 800 of these grants since 1994, ranging in value from $10,000 to $20,000.[50] EPA also has special programs to assist communities in monitoring and reducing pollution through its Environmental Justice Through Pollution Prevention (EJP2) program, which provided over $15 million for 198 grants from 1995 through 1999.[51]

EPA has several programs that aim to increase participation by low-income and minority groups.[52] For example, EPA translates documents into languages other than English and has released guidance for communities on how to get involved in the environmental permitting process. Guidance documents available include *Public Involvement in Environmental Permits: A Reference Guide* (August 2000), which was released after consultation with the NEJAC and the Environmental Council of States.

3.2.7 Department of Labor

This section describes the U.S. Department of Labor's efforts to implement environmental justice into its programs and operations. At the December 2000 meeting, Dr. Roland Droitsch, Deputy Assistant Secretary, Office of the Assistant Secretary for Policy, briefed NEJAC meeting on DOL's achievements.

Policies and Evaluation

No specific information concerning department-wide policies or evaluations of environmental justice was reported.

Organizational Investments

No specific organizational investments related to environmental justice were reported.

Programmatic Procedures

According to Dr. Droitsch, many of DOL's traditional programs and initiatives promote the goals of environmental justice, particularly those that provide employment and skills training. DOL has worked

---

[50] Binder, et al.

[51] Ibid.

[52] Ibid.

with the Partnership for Environmental Technology Education (PETE) to offer training opportunities to disadvantaged communities. Environmental technology, lead abatement, and hazardous waste cleanup are fields that offer a number of career opportunities, especially to communities that are subject to a disproportionate share of environmental dangers, said Dr. Droitsch. Enviro-jobs was another DOL program that Dr. Droitsch mentioned as being consistent with EJ objectives.

When asked about DOL's position on the disproportionate number of minorities that suffer from occupational illness and injury, Dr. Droitsch responded to the Executive Council that the Occupational Safety and Hazard Administration (OSHA), a division of DOL, has a targeted approach to handling such human health issues in the workplace. He reported that OSHA has identified the most dangerous work sites and the population segments that are prone to occupational illness and injury. Outside sources indicate that this concept has been implemented on a local level; for example, the North Carolina Department of Labor Research and Statistics Division maintains a database on occupational illnesses and injuries. The database contains the results of an on-going sample of all private-sector employees (except those in low-risk industries which qualify for the small employer exemption and employees in state and local government agencies). The North Carolina DOL also publishes *Occupational Illnesses and Injuries*, a booklet with information from the database, which is categorized by industry.[53]

External Outreach

Dr. Droitsch also reported that DOL participated in the National Training Collaborative for Environmental Justice, as well as several IWG projects. For example, in the Bridges to Friendship Project, DOL collaborated with the Navy, community groups, and other federal agencies to work with at-risk youth in southeast Washington, D.C. by offering them life skills and job training, in addition to remediating the environmental contamination of their neighborhoods. Dr. Droitsch stressed the potential of this project to transform the Anacostia area in D.C.

3.2.8   National Institute of Environmental Health Sciences

This section presents the environmental justice programs within the National Institute of Environmental Health Sciences (NIEHS), an institute within the National Institute of Health at the U.S. Department of Health and Human Services. At the December NEJAC Meeting, Dr. Charles Wells, Director of Environmental Health Sciences at NIEHS, presented new NIEHS programs and policies developed in response to the EO 2898.

Policies and Evaluation

As stated on the NIEHS website, the mission of NIEHS is to "reduce the burden of human illness and dysfunction from environmental causes by understanding each of these elements and how they interrelate." The NIEHS achieves its mission through research programs, prevention and intervention efforts, and community outreach, training, and technological transfer.[54] According to Dr. Wells, NIEHS has changed its policy and has worked to implement strategies in all of its programs to empower people in communities who are victims of environmental injustices. He also noted that NIEHS is presently the only institute within NIH that has the responsibility for addressing environmental justice, although other institutes are beginning to get involved. The ELI article indicates that NIEHS participated in the development of the overall HHS environmental justice strategy, and developed its own Strategic Plan 2000, which includes environmental justice initiatives.[55] And although not addressed in Dr. Wells'

---

[53] http://www.ibiblio.org/hass/R_6.1.1._govt.html.

[54] http://www.niehs.nih.gov/external/intro.htm.

[55] Binder, et al.

presentation, NIEHS regularly evaluates the work of its grantees and has conducted an evaluation of its total environmental justice program.[56]

Organizational Investments

Dr. Wells did not specifically address organizational investments made by the NIEHS, other than the expansion of its research programs, as addressed in the section below. However, the ELI article indicates that NIEHS has four professional staff and additional support staff primarily engaged in implementation of the Institute's environmental justice research programs.[57]

Programmatic Procedures

Dr. Wells noted that NIEHS has expanded its efforts to address disparities in adverse health effects among various populations. For example, he noted the following ways in which NIEHS has implemented environmental justice concerns into its research programs and prevention efforts:

- Focusing three of its eight environmental health research centers (located at academic institutions) on environmental justice issues, such as risks to agricultural workers.

- Redesigning and developing new asthma studies to address the risks of adverse respiratory health effects experienced by minority or disadvantaged children (e.g., in the inner city).

- Developing a clinical trial designed to address the issue of lead exposure in minority or disadvantaged communities, and identify solutions for removal of lead from exposed individuals. NIEHS is also examining the relationship between lead exposure and adverse effects such as low birth weight.

- Conducting research on adverse effects of environmental toxics (e.g., PCBs, mercury, lead, and fluorides) to which Native American children are exposed through their diet.

External Outreach

In his presentation, Dr. Wells indicated that NIEHS conducts an outreach program that educates scientists on the importance of developing knowledge of the populations with which they are working. He also described several NIEHS projects that focus on providing minority and disadvantaged populations with information to address potential health concerns:

- Developing a community-based research project that focuses on disadvantaged and underserved populations exposed to environmental contaminants. The project, which has nine grantees, works to implement culturally relevant prevention and intervention activities in these communities.

- Developing the "Environmental Justice: Partnership for Communication" program, which provides grants to help populations who are at risk of exposure to get involved in decision-making about NIEHS research that affects them.

- Maintaining a job training program for minority and inner-city youth, educating them to identify and address environmental problems in their own communities.

---

[56] Ibid.

[57] Ibid.

- Increasing the number of minority individuals involved in the research of environmental health.

3.2.9 Health Resources and Services Administration

This section presents the environmental justice activities of the Health Resources and Services Administration (HRSA) at the U.S. Department of Health and Human Services, as presented by Dr. Hubert Avant, Director for Urban Health, in the Bureau of Primary Health Care at HRSA.

Policies and Evaluation

The mission of HRSA, according to their website, is to ensure equitable access to comprehensive, quality health care across the nation.[58] In his presentation, Dr. Avant observed that integrated health care delivery is crucial for underserved communities, and indicated that the mission of his Bureau, going forward, is to increase access to health care and improve the health status of such populations.

Organizational Investments

No specific information was provided about internal organizational investments to implement environmental justice activities and program.

Programmatic Procedures

In his presentation, Dr. Avant identified several recent programs in which HRSA is using existing program infrastructures to address the health care of underserved populations. Specifically, HRSA is currently funding more than 800 community health centers, which are required to provide care – from prenatal to gerontological life stages – in order to receive their funding. In 1998, HRSA entered into a memorandum of understanding with ATSDR to implement strategies for enhancing environmental medicine in the HRSA community health center program. This will provide training to providers not only in these centers but also those who work with HRSA to deliver services around the country.

External Outreach

Dr. Avant noted that HRSA enters into partnerships with external organizations to use existing community infrastructures for conducting outreach to communities. For example, HRSA is entering into contracts with community action agencies such as Meals on Wheels and Head Start to disseminate health information. Also, HRSA recently entered into an agreement with CDC to develop the Community Health Outreach and Educational Services Program, which will use community health centers to disseminate information about disparities in adverse health effects among various populations.

3.2.10 Agency for Toxic Substances and Disease Registry

This section presents the environmental justice activities of the Agency for Toxic Substances and Disease Registry (ATSDR) in the Centers for Disease Control and Prevention at the U.S. Department of Health and Human Services. The ATSDR presentation was made by Dr. Rueben Warren, Associate Administrator for Urban Affairs, at ATSDR.

Policies and Evaluation

---

[58] http://www.hrs.gov.

In his presentation, Dr. Warren stated that ATSDR is committed to working with the environmental justice community, and views environmental justice as a subset of public health, which is "social justice." Although he did not specifically address ATSDR policies, the Agency does have an environmental justice strategy (available on their website) that appears to provide the basis for ATSDR's environmental justice activities.[59] According to the strategy, the goal of ATSDR's environmental justice efforts is to assure that communities of concern are informed and involved in ATSDR activities related to the environment and environmental health. The strategy includes evaluation measures to assess how well environmental justice issues are addressed during implementation of ATSDR activities. These measures include an increase in the number of partnerships during planning stages, a reduction in the number of environmental justice complaints, and the development of improved strategies for interacting with residents of communities of concern.

Organizational Investments

Dr. Warren noted that ATSDR's structural commitment to environmental justice was evinced by its Office of Urban Affairs (OUA), which was established in 1997 to focus on environmental justice and minority health issues. According to the environmental justice strategy, the OUA works with other divisions and offices within ATSDR to develop and implement programs that address equity issues. Dr. Warren also noted that ATSDR had developed a diverse workforce.

Programmatic Procedures

Dr. Warren indicated that ATSDR utilizes its partnerships with other agencies (e.g., health departments and environmental quality departments) to establish functional mechanisms to implement its commitment to environmental justice.

External Outreach

Dr. Warren stated that ATSDR has made progress in learning to listen to environmental justice communities, and is working at the local level with communities and environmental justice organizations. ATSDR is also collaborating with five new programs in public health at Historically Black Colleges and Universities.

3.2.11 United States Department of Agriculture

This section presents the progress being made within the U.S. Department of Agriculture (USDA), as presented by Mr. Terry Harwood at the December NEJAC meeting, and from additional sources that provided explanatory details about USDA's environmental justice activities.

Policies and Evaluations

According to Mr. Harwood, USDA has established a formal policy that addresses environmental justice issues. Although Mr. Harwood did not outline the history of this policy, additional sources report that the policy was issued as part of a USDA departmental regulation (DR) promulgated on December 15, 1997 (DR 5600-2) to outline the USDA's strategy for implementing EO 12898.[60] The regulation includes a departmental policy to identify, mitigate, and prevent adverse human health or environmental

---

[59] http://www.atsdr.cdc.gov/OUA/ejstrategy.html.

[60] Binder, et al.

effects. It also commits USDA to providing opportunities for minority and low-income populations to participate in planning and decision-making on matters that affect their health or environment.[61]

Organizational Investments

Although Mr. Harwood did not specifically discuss organizational changes that USDA has undertaken to implement the EO, other sources have indicated how environmental justice responsibilities have been delegated within the Department. For example, the ELI article reports that the USDA's Under Secretary for Natural Resources and Environment has overall leadership responsibility for implementation of the EO. An Environmental Justice Steering Committee was formed to advise the Under Secretary both with regard to compliance with the EO and concerning effectiveness in addressing environmental justice issues. The Steering Committee is to meet twice yearly. Agency heads are also required to report annually to both the Under Secretary and the Steering Committee, detailing their practices and accomplishment toward ensuring compliance with the EO.[62] Progress on USDA program activities that incorporate environmental justice concerns are highlighted on some USDA websites.[63]

Programmatic Procedures

Mr. Harwood stated that the Department's policy is to work within existing environmental and other programmatic frameworks. For example, the Forest Service frequently incorporates environmental justice considerations in its decision-making under the NEPA process. Other sources report that additional policies, statutes, or regulations are used by other parts of the Department to address environmental justice for their specific programs, particularly those parts of the Department for which NEPA is not required.

Mr. Harwood reported that USDA addresses tribal environmental justice issues by emphasizing the participation of small and disadvantaged businesses in contracting and procurement programs for environmental cleanup projects. The Department approaches cleanups from two standpoints. First, according to Mr. Harwood, they are an enforcement agency for cleanup on contaminated public lands, where the Department has authority similar to EPA's. Second, as a natural resources trustee, the USDA works with states and tribes to clean up public lands that affect tribes. The Department also assists tribes (as co-trustees with tribal governments) on cleanup projects on tribal lands, and hires Indian-owned firms to conduct cleanup. The Department also helps tribes with the natural resource damage assessment process. The USDA recently negotiated an MOU in Idaho, an area of considerable phosphate mining. The area is contaminated with selenium, and the tribes, DOI, USDA, EPA, and the state have signed onto a single MOU that outlines the management of cleanup of an extensive area, including the role that tribes will play in the cleanup. Mr. Harwood also reported that USDA is working with tribes in some post-treatment areas in the Great Lakes, as well as a site in Nevada in which a tribe is being affected by downstream contamination.

External Outreach

Many of the projects that demonstrate USDA's commitment involve external outreach and coordination with or support to state and local programs. This section highlights recent outreach and coordination projects. In his presentation, Mr. Harwood provided brief descriptions of the projects that are outlined below. Additional sources provided more detail about each project. Although Mr. Harwood did not have time during his presentation to specifically mention the Services within USDA that performed

---

[61] Ibid.

[62] Ibid.

[63] For example, www.usda.gov/oce/smallfarm/actions/goal8act.htm provides insight into the Small Farms' program and its progress with respect to EJ issues.

these activities, the USDA website and other sources were consulted for additional information about each project and the Services that have undertaken them.

- Natural Resource Conservation Service (NRCS) – According to Mr. Harwood, USDA collaborates with other federal agencies, state and local governments, and public and private organizations to provide grants and technical assistance to minority and low-income urban communities to accomplish urban ecosystem conservation through locally driven initiatives. He cited two examples; another source clarified that these projects were undertaken by NRCS.[64] USDA provided funds to the members of the Cleveland Minority Environmental Association's Earth Day and water quality testing program, and also provided funds to the National Coalition to Restore Urban Waterways to develop guidelines for restoration of urban waterways by training urban community groups. According to another source, additional efforts undertaken by NRCS include providing funding for a cooperative agreement with Tuskegee University to develop guidelines for implementing an environmental justice policy, and funding of a research initiative to gather information on potential environmental justice issues through the Southern Food Systems Education Consortium.[65]

- Rural Utilities Service – Mr. Harwood highlighted USDA's support for Brownfields Showcase Communities; additional resources stated that this program is largely supported by USDA Rural Development loans for infrastructure. The Brownfields Showcase program focuses attention on rural, minority, or tribal communities that can benefit from programs that have historically highlighted large inner city industrial sites. Mr. Harwood noted that USDA has successfully helped two communities with their applications to get signed up for the showcase program: Cape Charles, Virginia and Metlakatla, Alaska. The EPA Brownfields Showcase website[66] provided more insight into the results of this support. Cape Charles, Virginia, is predominantly an African-American community that has succeeded in creating the nation's first eco-industrial park. Metlakatla, Alaska, is the remotely located home of the Metlakatla Indian Community, a federally designated Enterprise Community. This community is promoting sustainable economic development through brownfields cleanup and redevelopment while restoring and protecting the community's natural resources.[67] Another source cited NRCS' support of *Water 2000*, a partnership between USDA's Rural Utilities Services, other federal, state and local agencies, foundations, and private lenders, which seeks to provide targeted loans, grants and technical assistance to improve small community and colonias water systems.[68] The goal is to bring the systems into compliance with the Safe Drinking Water Act.[69]

- Forest Service (USFS) – Mr. Harwood commented that USDA assists minority and low-income urban communities to accomplish urban ecosystem conservation through locally-driven initiatives. Although Mr. Harwood did not specifically cite this example, another source highlighted the USFS and its support to the Urban Tree House

---

[64] Binder, et al.

[65] Ibid.

[66] http://www.epa.gov/swerosps/bf/.

[67] Ibid.

[68] Colonias are low-income developments along the US-Mexico border that often lack adequate sewer systems, water services, housing, and other critical services.

[69] Binder, et al.

Program. Under the Urban Tree House Program, the USDA committed itself to working with community residents in the Naval District and Southeast Washington, D.C.; East Atlanta, Georgia; Chicago, Illinois; and Midcity, Louisiana. According to this source, the goal of the Urban Tree House is to provide opportunities for environmental education in urban settings, and particularly in communities who may not have the chance for such learning through formal and other nonformal programs.[70] The Urban Tree House process brings together partners -- including federal, state, and local governments, local community groups, for-profit organizations, business, and industry, non-profit organizations, and individuals -- with compatible objectives related to urban environmental education.[71]

- Animal and Plant Health Inspection Service (APHIS) -- Mr. Harwood reported that USDA supports cooperative agreements with state agencies to participate in pest eradication efforts, which involve evaluation and communication of health risks due to pesticide application. An additional source[72] highlights specific activities that APHIS undertakes in support of this effort. For example, APHIS translates documents pertaining to pesticide impacts on health for Non-English speaking populations. APHIS' Texas Lower Rio Grande Boll Weevil Eradication program translated documents into Spanish and had translators available at public meetings for farm workers and their families. Many food safety publications and videos are also available in Spanish.[73]

- Cooperative State Research, Education and Extension Service (CSREES – Mr. Harwood noted that USDA responds to the needs of industrial and field workers for health protection through cotton dust control, grain dust reduction, and safe pesticide application technology as well as dissemination of safe pesticide handling information. He also mentioned that USDA collects, maintains and analyzes information on the consumption patterns of populations who principally rely on fish and wildlife for subsistence. According to another source,[74] the CSREES is the Service within USDA that performs these various activities. For example, CSREES communicates to the public regarding the health risks of consumption patterns, including the consumption of wildlife for subsistence. In addition, this source reports that fact sheets and bulletins are disseminated through the Extension Service delivery system to appropriate target populations. Mr. Harwood also mentioned USDA's support for state and local involvement in integrated pest management strategies and in setting priorities setting for research, education and regulatory controls; according to the external source,[75] this work is conducted primarily by CSREES.

3.2.12 Housing and Urban Development

This section presents the efforts and progress made by the U.S. Department of Housing and Urban Development (HUD) in carrying out environmental justice measures that satisfy EO 12898. At the December NEJAC Meeting, the following presentations were made:

---

[70] Ibid.

[71] http://www.fs.fed.us/research/rvur/urban/urbantreehouse/uthouse.htm.

[72] Binder, et al.

[73] http://www.aphis.usda.gov/oa/pubs.html.

[74] Binder, et al.

[75] Ibid.

- Mr. Marvin Wentz Turner, Special Actions Office, Office of the Secretary distributed a fact sheet on HUD's environmental justice initiatives to the Executive Council.

- Ms. Antoinette Sebastian, Senior Environmental Policy Analyst, and Mr. Robert McAlpine, Special Assistant to the Assistant Secretary, presented and commented on a handout that summarized the actions that HUD has taken to incorporate environmental justice into its policies, programs, and activities. The handout was given to the members of the Air and Water Subcommittee.

- Ms. Betsy A. Ryan, Senior Equal Opportunity Specialist, Office of Fair Housing and Equal Opportunity, reported HUD's progress in enforcement activities to the Enforcement Subcommittee.

- Mr. James Floyd, Office of Public and Indian Housing, during a presentation to the NEJAC Indigenous Peoples Subcommittee, explained how HUD's outreach programs have reached Native American tribes.

Policies and Evaluation

Although not explicitly stated in its mission statement, according to Ms. Sebastian, HUD developed a strategy on environmental justice that is based on three principles: (1) housing policies that are environmentally sound, preserve affordability, and promote economic growth and investment; (2) the environmental quality of public housing and programs that offer low-income and minority populations a safe and healthy opportunity for self-sufficiency; and (3) a redesign of its programs and services, using an environmental justice framework, to empower citizens to take action and improve their own lives.

Organizational Investments

Although HUD has not assigned personnel to work full-time on environmental justice matters, the agency has delegated such responsibilities to several individuals. Staff members of the Community Planning Office and in the Office of Fair Housing and Equal Opportunity have devoted a percentage of their time to the environmental justice aspects of projects.

In terms of training, the handout presented to the Air and Water Subcommittee also listed four HUD-conducted sessions on Title VI to approximately 160 compliance investigators. Furthermore, for its Native American programs, HUD has offered training specifically for environmental clearances that are stipulated under the Native American Housing and Self- Determination Act of 1996.

Programmatic Procedures

A major component of the handout presented to the Air and Water Subcommittee by Ms. Sebastian was a draft guide developed by HUD that establishes a protocol for the investigation of environmental justice complaints. Complaints are often grounded in Title VI, Title VIII (prohibits discrimination relating to housing) and Section 109 of Title 1 of the Housing and Community Development Act of 1974 (prohibits racial discrimination by recipients of the HUD community development block grant). According to Ms. Ryan, presently HUD has received 675 complaints—12 of them relating to environmental justice issues. Interagency cooperation will help HUD respond to these complaints more promptly, said Ms. Ryan.

Furthermore, HUD has primarily integrated environmental justice considerations into four of their existing programs: empowerment zones and enterprise communities (EZ/EC), combating lead-based paint poisoning, brownfield redevelopment, and colonias.[76]

- Empowerment Zones and Empowerment Communities (EZ/EC) -- Ms. Sebastian highlighted HUD's commitment to ensuring that low-income individuals and minorities enjoy safe and healthy living conditions. This is manifested in HUD's EZ/EC program, which funds low-income neighborhoods that suffer from unemployment and other social ailments. In accordance with EO 12898, HUD has integrated environmental justice considerations in the allocation and planning processes for ECs. For example, residents of an EC in Chicago will be hired by HUD to help clean up 25 contaminated acres of land in their community.[77]

- Combating Lead-Based Paint Poisoning -- During her presentation, Ms. Sebastian emphasized the danger of lead-based paint to residents of low-income housing, especially children, and how HUD has dedicated numerous resources to combating it. HUD's lead paint initiative also fulfills the requirements of the Residential Lead-Based Paint Hazard Protection Act of 1992.[78] Throughout its efforts, HUD has conducted lead testing in approximately 95% of the nation's public housing built before 1978.[79] To implement Title X of the Housing and Community Development Act of 1992, HUD organized a 39-member Task Force that issued a series of recommendations reflecting the opinions of many experts in the field on how to ensure lead-safe homes without driving up the cost of affordable housing.[80] Under its grant program, HUD requires that its grantees provide lead education programs for its residents. $279 million has been awarded to state and local governments to reduce lead hazards in private, low-income housing, and grantees can choose which hazard control methods are most effective in their own communities.

- Brownfield Redevelopment -- Brownfields, abandoned property where re-expansion is hindered by real or perceived environmental contamination,[81] have led to the decline of many low-income urban areas in the U.S. HUD and EPA undertook a joint research effort to investigate whether potential environmental contamination discourages investment. HUD is also working with lawmakers to develop a new Community Development Block Grant (CDBG) Fund, which will enable communities to organize cleanup efforts of brownfields as well as redevelopment activities.

- Colonias -- Colonias are low-income developments along the US-Mexico border that often lack adequate sewer systems, water services, housing, and other critical services. HUD has mandated that certain states -- including Arizona, California, New Mexico, and Texas -- designate a certain percentage of their CDBG funds to address such problems that colonias face. HUD has also allocated funds from Section 8 of the Community Investment Demonstration (Pension Fund Program) to support three

---

[76] Binder, et al.

[77] Ibid.

[78] Ibid.

[79] "U.S. Department of Housing and Urban Development, A Commitment to Communities: Achieving Environmental Justice." www.hud.gov/cpd/ocv/ejreport.html.

[80] Ibid.

[81] Ibid.

multifamily housing programs in the Colonias region. This includes the Azteca project, which provides for the construction of 50 units of Section 8 rental housing for low-income families and individuals.

- Native American Programs -- HUD has also expanded or created new programs to work with Native American tribes, serving as a liaison between them and other federal agencies. Mr. Floyd discussed the Native American Housing and Self-Determination Act (NAHASDA), a 1996 law that merged several independent assistance programs into a single block grant program that is more manageable. According to Mr. Floyd, NAHASDA gives tribes greater discretion in their housing policy decisions.

External Outreach

HUD reportedly had extensive outreach efforts well before EO 12898 was promulgated. For example, community education is an integral part of HUD's lead program. By providing educational materials in several languages and tailoring them to be culturally sensitive, HUD attempts to ensure that information on lead abatement and safety reaches a diverse audience. For example, "Protect Your Family," a pamphlet sponsored by HUD and EPA, is written in Spanish.[82] HUD has also started using its Community 2020 Software, which is a geographic information system that can identify at-risk minority and low-income populations and further identifies the risks that are the most threatening to those populations.[83]

Ms. Sebastian recommended that the committee visit HUD's website for more information on its outreach programs. HUD's website features "A Commitment to Communities: Achieving Environmental Justice," a report that notes that HUD provided technical assistance to many community development efforts around the country. For example, HUD provided assistance in revitalizing Altgeld Gardens, a public housing development in Chicago that is surrounded by hazardous operations and waste treatment facilities. HUD has lent similar support to public housing developments in Southeast Washington, D.C. and East St. Louis.

3.2.13 Department of State and United States Trade Representative's Office

While neither the Department of State nor the United States Trade Representative's Office (USTR) were requested to participate in this Council meeting, largely because they were not designated as members of the Interagency Working Group by the Executive Order No. 12898 on Environmental Justice, NEJAC's International Subcommittee requested that both entities be included in this Report.

The relevance of the work of both of these entities has become increasingly important to international environmental justice issues in recent years. In particular, the 1999 "Roundtable on Environmental Justice Issues on the U.S./Mexico Border" (Border Roundtable), sponsored by the NEJAC International Subcommittee and EPA in San Diego, California (August 19-21, 1999), made clear that there are significant pollution and other environmental issues affecting low-income, minority, and indigenous populations along the U.S./Mexico border area. Some of these impacts have been attributed to transboundary pollution and the economic effects of the North American Free Trade Agreement in attracting significant economic and industrial development to both sides of the border area. At the same time, recent work by the NEJAC with regard to the effects of U.S. government-assisted efforts of pesticide spraying in pursuit of destruction of drug crops ("Plan Colombia") and the associated health and subsistence-ability impacts on poor local and indigenous communities have demonstrated the international aspects of environmental justice in other countries.

---

[82] Ibid.

[83] Ibid.

These issues are symptomatic of the increasing importance of environmental justice issues that are of a transboundary and international nature. It has also given rise to a greater need for participation and involvement of both the State Department and USTR environmental justice issues. More importantly, EPA's efforts alone in this regard will likely be insufficient without the cooperation and assistance of other parts of the federal government involved in decision-making and policy-setting regarding transboundary and international issues. Yet neither of these agencies is explicitly covered by the EO. To the extent that their programs, policies and activities cause adverse environmental impacts on low-income, minority, and indigenous populations in the United States, such programs, policies, and activities would clearly fall within the scope of activities that the EO was intended and designed to address. In fact, commendably, the State Department itself has recognized that it has obligations under EO 12898 -- it requires that an analysis of environmental justice issues be part of the permitting process for facilities on the U.S./Mexico Border. In the end, what is most important for the resolution of environmental justice issues at the border and elsewhere internationally are not discussions about the semantics of the EO but consideration of the substantive goals and purposes that the EO seeks to achieve - environmental justice for low-income, minority, and indigenous populations.

However, neither entity has prepared an Environmental Justice Strategy nor has either participated in the Interagency Working Group on Environmental Justice. To promote increased attention by these agencies to environmental justice issues, in November 1999, the NEJAC Executive Council adopted a Resolution calling for EPA to involve the State Department and the USTR more closely in the work of the Interagency Working Group on Environmental Justice and on environmental justice issues more generally. It also recommended that EPA seek their official designation by the Executive Order No. 12898 on Environmental Justice as members of the Interagency Working Group.

While these agencies have not been designated as official Interagency Working Group members, through the efforts of EPA's Office of International Activities, staff of the State Department and USTR have engaged in discussions with the NEJAC International Subcommittee about the relationship of their work to international and transboundary environmental justice issues as well as opportunities to address such issues in their work. The initial willingness of these entities to engage in discussions has been encouraging. However, it is important that these agencies continue to be involved in environmental justice issues given the increasing importance of such concerns internationally. In this regard, the International Subcommittee recommends that EPA's Office of International Activities continue to seek the involvement of both the State Department and USTR in environmental justice issues that are of a transboundary or international nature.

3.3   Analysis of Federal Agency Progress in Implementing Environmental Justice

As the information presented in Section 3.2 indicates, individual federal agencies have demonstrated varying levels of progress in integrating environmental justice principles in their day-to-day operations. The purpose of this section is to present an overall picture of federal progress, and highlight common themes and individual agency achievements. At the end of this section is a table, entitled *Summary of Environmental Justice Efforts in Federal Agency Programs,* that summarizes the environmental justice efforts reviewed for this report.

Policies and Evaluations

As discussed in the functional framework in Section 3.1, senior level support is a crucial factor in ensuring the success of an environmental justice program. Such support can be manifested in agency-wide policies or strategies that lay the groundwork for implementation of the program. Nearly every agency reported having some type of policy or strategy for implementing environmental justice within the organization, with the exception of the Department of Labor. In some cases, the policies are formalized in stand-alone documents (and may be publicly available on the agency's website), while in other cases similar policy concepts are presented within the agency's overall operating plan. For large, compartmentalized agencies such as DOD and DOI, the policies are developed within the individual services or bureaus.

In general, while having an environmental justice policy is evidence of progress, whether the agency is actually following the plan depends on organizational investments and programmatic procedures, such as discussed below. However, it should be noted that one additional measure of commitment is whether an agency has an evaluation process that examines how well the agency is actually implementing the policies set forth. Only NIEHS has reported conducting an evaluation or assessment of their environmental justice efforts, although ATSDR includes evaluation measures in its overall strategy. No other agencies provided evidence of such evaluations of progress in environmental justice program implementation.

Organizational Investments

No agency can successfully implement its environmental justice program without providing the necessary resources to carry it out. A number of agencies have created offices or staff positions for overseeing or coordinating environmental justice efforts within the department. For example, like EPA's Office of Environmental Justice, ATSDR established the Office of Urban Affairs to implement its programs. DOJ and DOE have established environmental justice contacts in each major department. NIEHS indicated that it has four staff persons dedicated to environmental justice research program implementation. Other agencies, such as DOD and HUD, have assigned environmental justice responsibilities to existing staff rather than create new positions. Either model can be effective provided that the office or individuals assigned the responsibility have the authority and resources to carry them out.

In addition to assigning specific responsibilities for implementation, some agencies (e.g., DOT, DOJ, DOE, and USDA) have created working groups or steering committees to guide implementation. The Department of Transportation, for example, created a review committee comprised of senior department officials to examine the impact of major transportation projects on minority and low-income communities. This formalized mechanism to promote sustained senior official attention to ongoing DOT activities is likely to have enhanced the incorporation of environmental justice considerations into the agency's key activities. However, from most of the department and agency reports, it is unclear to what the degree these positions have an ability to influence or create measurably positive results for environmental justice.

Programmatic Procedures

EO 12898 requires that each agency take environmental justice into account in its day-to-day operations and decision-making. Nearly every agency and department reports incorporating environmental justice criteria into its NEPA procedures and guidance. This integration is particularly important for those agencies, such as DOT, DOD, and DOE, that undertake activities that can have significant environmental impacts, such as locating a highway, disposing of chemical weapons, or cleaning up nuclear production facilities. Even DOJ has incorporated environmental justice considerations into guidance for completing environmental assessments in building prisons. Furthermore, DOT has incorporated environmental justice criteria into planning requirements that states and metropolitan planning organizations (MPOs) must follow. DOT has also established an environmental justice data bank to track environmental justice issues across department activities.

Those agencies that are not necessarily involved in environmental decision-making still developed procedures and guidelines for ensuring that environmental justice concepts are incorporated into the activities that they do implement. For example, HUD has developed a protocol for investigating environmental justice complaints. NIEHS redirected some of its health research programs to ensure that environmental justice communities and their concerns were taken into account.

Stakeholder Outreach

From the presentations made at the NEJAC meeting, it appears that most agencies consider outreach to and interaction with communities of concern to be an important component of an environmental justice program. Nearly every department and agency reported at least a basic level of stakeholder outreach to minority and low-income communities. Some programs, such as DOE's environmental justice research center and NIEHS's Partnership for Communication, are intended to make technical information available to the public. Other agencies have established procedures to encourage public participation in decision-making; for example, DOJ seeks community input in approving environmental projects that resolve environmental prosecutions. Still other programs focus on training and job development, such as DOI's Job Corps centers.

Outreach is particularly important for those agencies that are not generally responsible for activities that have a direct effect on the environment. In the absence of being able to integrate environmental justice concepts into environmental decisions, these agencies have identified ways in which they can leverage their existing programs to assist communities of concern. For example, HUD targets outreach on lead exposure to high-risk populations. HRSA has created community health outreach programs to disseminate health care information to communities of concern.

To some degree, there is an element of "re-packaging" of existing outreach efforts to these stakeholders and casting those activities under the aegis of "environmental justice." For example, DOD's Restoration Advisory Boards and Technical Assistance programs had existed prior to the EO but are still presented as "environmental justice outreach." However, the degree to which the agency has enhanced stakeholder involvement as a result of the EO is unclear.

Summary

In attempting to provide an overall picture of federal progress in meeting the objectives of the EO, the agencies were assigned into one of four categories based on their "environmental footprint," as illustrated in the graphic below. An "environmental footprint" refers to the potential for negative impacts of agency activities on the environment. Agencies with large environmental footprints have historically been those whose activities directly generate hazardous or toxic substances and wastes, have emissions into air or water, or require the disturbance of significant tracts of land for buildings, transportation infrastructure, etc. Agencies with smaller environmental footprints tend to have far fewer activities that generate emissions or wastes, and rarely undertake activities that potentially damage the natural environment. In addition, both types of agencies may have statutory or regulatory authority over private or non-federal agency activities that impact the environment. Other agencies may have negligible environmental impacts as well as minimal responsibilities over such impacts.

Environmental Footprint

Large	Small

Environmental Protection Responsibility	High	DoD DOE DOT USDA	DOI EPA DOJ
	Low		DOL HUD NIEHS HRSA ATSDR

Although one might expect that agencies with larger environmental footprints and high environmental responsibilities would have mature programs to incorporate environmental justice into their operations, this does not appear to be the case. For example, based on the information provided in the presentations and from research into each agency, it appears that NIEHS and DOT have relatively strong efforts to incorporate environmental justice into their agency activities and programs. However, other agencies such as DoD and DOE do not have strong environmental justice programs, despite their large environmental footprints. While these two large agencies may have pockets of excellence, their overall efforts are comparatively weaker.

Summary of Environmental Justice Efforts in Federal Agency Programs

	Policies and Evaluations	Organizational Investments	Programmatic Procedures	External Outreach
DOJ	• Created environmental justice strategy and guidance documents-but implementation left to discretion of individual attorneys. • Focus on specific problems whose resolution incorporates environmental justice.	• Environmental justice contacts in major offices. • Training provided to new hires. • Two working groups created to guide Department implementation.	• Incorporated environmental justice considerations into guidance for completing EA/EIS in corrections program.	• Seek community input to resolution of environmental cases through supplemental environmental projects. • Weed and Seed program incorporates environmental justice on pilot basis at 4 sites.
DOD	• Environmental justice included in DoD NEPA policy (DoD Instruction 4715.9). • Each Service has included environmental justice in its NEPA policy. • Environmental justice in environmental and planning guidance for each Service. • American Indian and Alaska Native Policy.	• Environmental justice Training video • Native American and Alaskan Natives - sensitivity training. • No additional staff in ODUSD(IE) - staff cover environmental justice as additional workload.	• NEPA decision-making process.	• Restoration Advisory Boards for cleanup (active and closed installations). • Technical Assistance for Public Participation program to give training to public.
DOE	• Environmental justice strategy with four goals.	• Appointed environmental justice coordinator. • Designated environmental justice points of contact. • Established tribal liaison. • Established implementation steering committee.	• Incorporating environmental justice into Superfund cleanups and NEPA process. • Providing energy resources to Native Americans. • Conducting health assessments.	• Developed environmental justice resource center. • Established People of Color and Disenfranchised Communities Environmental Health Network (the Coalition).

Summary of Environmental Justice Efforts in Federal Agency Programs

	Policies and Evaluations	Organizational Investments	Programmatic Procedures	External Outreach
DOT	• 1999 FHWA and FTA memo on including environmental justice in MPO planning process. • FHWA / FTA rule on including environmental justice in MPO planning process (under consideration as of Dec 2000). • DOT Order 5610.2. • FHWA Order 6640.23.	• Environmental Justice Review Committee comprising senior DOT officials. • Workshops and training prepared by FHWA OCR.	• Planning requirements for states and MPOs incorporate environmental justice principles. • NEPA process requires consideration of environmental justice. • Established environmental justice data bank.	• Stakeholder involvement requirements during planning and construction process. • DOT review and oversight of state and local projects. • DOT involvement in settling litigation involved environmental justice stakeholders.
DOI	• Environmental Justice Strategy (1995). • Each bureau has its own implementing policies.	• Environmental justice coordinator for each bureau. • Primary responsibility rests with Director's Office of Environmental Policy and Compliance. • An individual in each of DOI's eight bureaus responsible for coordinating environmental justice issues, in addition to a staffer in the Solicitor's Office. Nine individuals, therefore, have environmental justice responsibilities. • Some bureaus have established offices that implement environmental justice.	• Guidance for subsistence taking of fish and wildlife on federal lands in Alaska. • NPS-12, guidance for implementation of the procedural requirements of NEPA. • FACA Advisory Committee to advise OSM on specific regulatory issues; committee members from States, Tribes, industry, and residents of coalfield regions, many of whom are low-income.	• Established Job Corps centers that train urban minority groups to restore wetlands, build nature trails, construct refuge facilities. • Partners for Cultural Diversity Program encouraged minorities to pursue natural resource careers. • Resource Apprenticeships Program (RAPS) provides work and educational experiences for minority and low-income high school and college students. • Prepare documents in Tribal languages, Japanese, Spanish; provide translators at meetings. • Incorporate public involvement from all potentially affected groups into all NEPA decisions; focus on encouraging involvement from minority, Tribal, low-income populations.
EPA Region 6	• Environmental Justice Strategy (1995). • Environmental justice included in NEPA compliance analysis. • Environmental justice grant evaluation to assess performance. • 1996 environmental justice implementation plan - also evaluated implementation of environmental justice Strategy.	• Office of Environmental Justice. • Office of Civil Rights. • Environmental justice coordinators in each HQ office and in each Region. • Regional OEnvironmental justices. • Environmental justice website. • Environmental justice grants. • EPA plays interagency coordination role. • Environmental justice Training Collaborative. • Pesticide safety training collaborative effort with industry and states.	• Environmental justice included in EPA's Clean Air Act § 309 reviews. • NEPA decision-making process.	• Materials published in languages other than English. • Guidance for EPA Assistance Recipients Administering Environmental Permitting Programs. • Pollution monitoring and reduction assistance programs. • Guidance for Investigating Title VI Administrative Complaints Challenging Permits.

Summary of Environmental Justice Efforts in Federal Agency Programs

	Policies and Evaluations	Organizational Investments	Programmatic Procedures	External Outreach
DOL	• No specific information provided.	• No specific information provided.	• Partnership for Environmental Technology Education (PETE). • Enviro-jobs.	• Participation in National Training Collaborative.
NIEHS	• Incorporates environmental justice into its overall mission and strategic plan; • Evaluates overall environmental justice program.	• Four staff dedicated to environmental justice research program implementation.	• Focuses 3 research centers on environmental justice issues. • Refocuses asthma studies. • Analyzing lead exposure. • Researching environmental impacts on Native American children.	• Developed community based research project with grantees. • Developed Partnership for Communication. • Maintains job training program for minority and inner-city youth.
HRSA	• No specific strategy, but environmental justice is part of overall mission to provide equitable health care.	• No specific information provided.	• Funding community health centers to ensure equitable health care. • With CDC, developing community health outreach and education services program.	• Created community health outreach and educational services program to disseminate health care information.
ATSDR	• Has an environmental justice strategy on website; includes evaluation measures.	• Created Office of Urban Affairs to implement environmental justice programs.	• No information on specific programs .	• Works with communities – no specific information provided.
USDA	• Strategy outlined in Departmental regulation (DR 5600-2), December 15, 1997 .	• USDA Under Secretary for Natural Resources and Environment has overall leadership responsibility for implementation. • Environmental justice Steering Committee advises Under Secretary on compliance and effectiveness in addressing environmental justice issues. • Agency heads report annually to both the Under Secretary and Steering Committee, outlining progress on environmental justice.	• Bureaus within USDA use NEPA and other requirements as opportunity to incorporate environmental justice into decisions. • Emphasizes participation of small and disadvantaged businesses in contracting and procurement programs for environmental cleanup projects.	• Provide grants and technical assistance to minority and low-income urban communities to accomplish urban ecosystem conservation through locally driven initiatives. • Fund cooperative agreement to develop guidelines for implementing an environmental justice policy. • Fund research initiative to gather information on potential environmental justice issues . • Provide support to Brownfields projects that involve minority, Tribal, low-income populations.
HUD	• Developed environmental justice strategy.	• Delegated environmental justice responsibilities to staff members.	• Developed protocol for investigating environmental justice complaints. • Incorporated environmental justice concerns into 4 existing programs.	• Targets outreach on lead exposure to high risk populations.

4.   INTERAGENCY COLLABORATION

The accomplishments of the Interagency Working Group on Environmental Justice (IWG) provide a focal point for evaluating federal agency progress in implementing environmental justice objectives. The IWG was established under EO 12898 to provide a mechanism for ensuring that federal agencies meet the EO objectives. In May 2000, the IWG released the "Integrated Federal Interagency Environmental Justice Action Agenda" to promote the integration of environmental justice in the policies, programs, and activities of all federal agencies.[84]

At the December NEJAC meeting, a panel session focused on the IWG and its Action Agenda. Mr. Tim Fields (Assistant Administrator for Solid Waste and Emergency Response, EPA) explained that the Action Agenda provides a framework that assists federal agencies in developing and expanding collaborative federal environmental justice initiatives. Mr. Charles Lee stated that the Action Agenda should accomplish the following:

- Promote federal support of solutions that begin in communities and remain in communities;

- Link the federal, state, and local governments with community-based comprehensive planning processes;

- Seek collaboration and integration so that resources can be better targeted and leveraged;

- Develop a template for holistic community-based solutions to environmental justice issues; and

- Serve as a platform for advocating a new way of conducting business.

Under the Action Agenda, 15 interagency environmental justice demonstration projects have been initiated. At the NEJAC meeting, a separate panel discussion was devoted to presenting the successes and lessons learned of 6 of the 15 interagency environmental justice projects. These demonstration projects provide examples of federal interagency and agency-specific initiatives to build constructive partnerships with state, tribal, and local governments and environmental justice communities. Mr. Fields suggested that the Action Agenda and demonstration projects would provide the baseline from which environmental justice and community involvement and participation will be measured. He stated that he anticipated that the demonstration projects would evolve into a full-fledged program and provide a guide to the way in which the federal government should deal with other stakeholders in addressing environmental justice issues.

4.1   Examples of Interagency Collaboration

In their presentation, the representatives of six demonstration projects tended to focus on the role of the community in the demonstration projects, rather than on federal agency accomplishments. The common theme running through all of the presentations was that community control and input into decisions, with the support of federal agencies, is vital for success in the resolution of environmental justice issues.

- Bridges to Friendship -- Rear Admiral Chris Weaver presented an overview of the Bridges to Friendship project that is underway at the Washington Navy Yard in

---

[84] "An Integrated federal Interagency Environmental Justice Action Agenda," May 15, 2000 (pre-publication copy).

southeast Washington, D.C. RADM Weaver stressed the commitment of the Navy to improving the environmental situation at the Washington Navy Yard through environmental cleanup and increasing opportunities for the local residents to become involved. He highlighted the factors behind the success of the project by stating that it provides ways to combine the efforts of community groups, the Navy, other federal agencies, private individuals, the local community, and the District of Columbia. RADM Weaver cited the project partners' ability to link job needs with job opportunities as a major factor in building community pride in redevelopment and environmental cleanup at the Navy Yard.

- Bethel New Life Power Park -- Ms. Mary Nelson (Bethel New Life, Inc.) described the Bethel New Life Power Park demonstration project in Chicago, Illinois. She stated that Bethel is very fortunate to have a partnership with the Department of Energy's Argonne National Laboratory. She identified that the lessons learned from the project pointed to three key ingredients for a successful community redevelopment project. These are vision, the development of partnerships, and the use of an asset-based approach.

- Community Cleanup and Revitalization, Arkwright/Forest Park -- Mayor James Talley of the City of Spartanburg, South Carolina, presented a description of the Community Cleanup and Revitalization project in the Arkwright/Forest Park community of south side Spartanburg. Mayor Talley stated that two Superfund sites are located near the community and he described other local sites of environmental concern. He described how a partnership of EPA, NEJAC, city and local officials, a Senator and Congressman, and the local community have come together in a collaborative effort to develop a plan for the area and to overcome the barrier of cost to redevelopment. Mayor Talley stressed the importance of community involvement and control. He explained that if the project is under the control of the local community, it will remain focused on providing benefits to the community.

- Addressing Asthma in Puerto Rico -- Dr. José Rodríguez-Santana of the Asthma Coalition of Puerto Rico gave a presentation describing the project to address asthma in Puerto Rico. He stated that this was the first asthma project funded by federal agencies with the objective of reducing asthma among native Puerto Ricans. He described the involvement of EPA, HRSA, and HHS and relayed how they have collaborated with local health care providers and community groups to improve understanding of asthma in Puerto Rico. Mr. Lee stated that the involvement of HRSA has been important in demonstrating to that agency the importance of environmental justice, and in increasing understanding within the agency of larger environmental justice issues in which they can play a role.

- New Madrid County Tri-community Child Health Champion Campaign -- Dr. Emil Jason (Great Rivers Alliance of Natural Resource Districts) gave a presentation on the New Madrid County Tri-Community Child Health Champion Campaign in Missouri. He stated that the partners to the project included the Natural Resource Conservation Service of the USDA and EPA Region VII. He said the purpose of the project is to provide a safer environment for children by promoting community awareness of environmental health hazards and improving the ability of local communities to address concerns. Dr. Jason stated that the partnership between federal agencies, state agencies, local organizations, and the communities had been successful in meeting the project goals and objectives.

- <u>Protecting Children's Health and Reducing Lead Exposure</u> -- Dr. Richard Mark (Chief Executive Officer, East St. Louis Lead Project, St. Mary's Hospital, East St. Louis, Illinois) described the East St. Louis Lead Project. He explained the efforts to make the population more aware of the dangers of lead poisoning and the roles of some of the project partners. Dr. Mark explained that funding for the project has come from HUD, EPA, USACE, and USDA. The federal agencies have also been heavily involved in testing for lead in soils and housing and in educating the community.

In conclusion, Mr. Lee described his vision for a programmatic framework for the IWG. He identified six major items:

- Enhancing communications, training, and outreach;

- Instituting an evaluation methodology based on environmental justice principles;

- Developing and solidifying partnerships within, among, and outside the federal agencies;

- Identifying a set of cross-cutting themes for integrating environmental justice across federal agencies;

- Actively nurturing new demonstration projects; and

- Developing regional environmental justice integrated action plans.

4.2   Analysis of Interagency Collaboration

The examples of demonstration projects described above have certain common themes and lessons learned that can be translated into the Action Agenda and help build stronger environmental justice projects in the future. The demonstration projects were established to serve as living models to help federal agencies and stakeholder groups identify methods of improving interagency collaboration and achieving concrete benefits for environmental justice communities. The initial results of the demonstration projects have indicated that the partnership approach to problem solving, with a strong local community input into decision-making, is the key to success. The ability of affected communities to leverage federal resources and expertise and interact with federal, state, and local government agencies is firmly linked to the overall results of each demonstration project. Engaging community members and stakeholder organizations early in the decision-making process builds trust and leads to strong partnerships. Designation of a lead federal agency is also important because it provides a focal point for activity and removes the administrative and financial burden from the local community, which rarely possesses the resources to meet those demands.

The federal agencies charged with implementation of EO 12898 can use the demonstration projects as a means of promoting environmental justice within agency functions and as models from which to draw experience for new environmental justice challenges. Documenting the lessons learned from the demonstration projects will provide a guide to other communities and federal agencies in how best to approach environmental justice issues and reach consensus on actions that can address those issues. The continuation of the Action Agenda and its demonstration projects will provide a template for future environmental justice projects.

5.   CONCLUSIONS AND RECOMMENDATIONS

The presentations and discussions at the December 2000 NEJAC meeting demonstrate that the federal departments and agencies have made significant, but uneven, progress in implementing the requirements of EO 12898. Some agencies have more fully integrated environmental justice considerations into their activities and operations than others, and have demonstrated a strong commitment to promoting environmental justice. While other agencies have not demonstrated as much progress, they do show signs of some level of commitment and it is evident that no agency has completely failed to implement the Executive Order. While there are different degrees of environmental justice implementation, it appears that federal agencies with the greater potential for environmental justice impacts have at least focused some resources towards addressing environmental justice within their organizations.

Having been presented with this information, NEJAC recommends that the EPA and other federal agencies should:

1. Support advancement of the Interagency Working Group (IWG) Environmental Justice Action Agenda and its collaborative interagency problem-solving model as exemplified in the fifteen demonstration projects.

2. Continue individual agency-specific implementation of environmental justice.

    - Heavily impacted communities should be a priority under an agency's regular programs and enforcement initiatives.

    - High level officials should express support for environmental justice initiatives undertaken by agency rank and file. Employee incentives should be developed to promote such initiatives by rewarding employees for innovative ideas to address environmental justice.

    - EPA and other federal agencies should integrate environmental justice into strategic agency planning in order to better leverage resources and enhance environmental programs to achieve greater improvement in impacted communities.

    - EPA and other federal agencies should devote equitable resources towards achieving environmental justice, and should integrate environmental justice initiatives into all their respective programs to be implemented by each agency as part of its core mission.

    - EPA and other federal agencies should establish clear accountability for implementing environmental justice initiatives and establish effective public administration techniques for managers and staff to use in carrying out these responsibilities.

    - When there are potential environmental justice consequences to discrete (site-specific) agency actions, the federal agency with jurisdiction should use all means possible to bring affected community members into the regulatory processes at the earliest time possible and appropriate; this could include utilizing informal consultation before the onset of formal agency proceedings.

    - Federal agencies should develop evaluative criteria and scheduled, periodic evaluations of environmental justice initiatives. Those periodic reports should be made publically available. The EPA, as the agency identified to oversee implementation of the Executive Order No. 12898 on Environmental Justice, should call for periodic reports and updates on environmental justice strategies undertaken by the agencies.

- Federal agencies should include environmental justice representatives in all stakeholder fora that address issues having potentially adverse environmental effects on environmental justice communities. Stakeholders representation should include persons from communities likely to be directly affected by such impacts, or persons who work directly with such communities.

- EPA in particular should continue to seek the involvement of both the State Department and United States Trade Representative's office in environmental justice issues that are of a transboundary or international nature.

3. Explore and identify ways for greater use of legal authorities and removal of regulatory impediments to achieve environmental justice.

   - Federal agencies can take action that is consistent with both the existing statutes and the Executive Order. Federal agencies do not need to change their agency mission, and in many cases, the legislature will not have to amend or repeal any existing statutes prior to agency action to respond to environmental justice concerns.

   - Federal agencies should follow EPA's example in analyzing their enabling statutes and regulations to identify sources of authority, discretionary or otherwise, to help them better respond to environmental justice concerns. In particular, Federal agencies should revise existing regulations and guidance documents to either remove existing impediments or to better address environmental justice issues

   - Environmental justice should be addressed at the programmatic level, for example, all agency rules, regulations and guidance documents should include explicit environmental justice protections to reduce the risk of adverse impacts to environmental justice communities.

4. Ensure that, in the case of federally-recognized tribes including Alaska Native villages, integration of environmental justice into agency policies, programs, and activities is consistent with the federal trust responsibility to tribes, recognized principles of tribal sovereignty, and the government-to-government relationship with tribes. More specifically, NEJAC incorporates by reference the further recommendations specific to tribes and Indian country developed by its Indigenous Peoples Subcommittee and attached hereto as Appendix A.

5. Collaborate in identifying specific focus areas or target programs where application of environmental justice principles could significantly benefit communities.

   - EPA should identify and communicate to sister agencies specific projects or tasks within their individual missions and jurisdiction which, if prioritized, undertaken or conducted, would have specific benefits to environmental justice communities. This should include identification of actions or programs otherwise scheduled which could be refocused on either a geographic or substantive sector basis to environmental justice communities.

   - EPA should specifically work with the federal health related agencies to identify ways to enhance the collection of health related data in and from environmental justice communities; identify specific research needs related to health issues prevalent in environmental justice communities; and identify opportunities for health related intervention in environmental justice communities.

- EPA should work with the federal health related agencies to identify and achieve a better understanding of the particular health vulnerabilities or sensitivities experienced among environmental justice community groups and evaluate mechanisms to address documented concerns, including but not limited to, provision of specific services and regulatory relief.

The NEJAC's first recommendation stems from the information presented in Section 4 of this report, which presents a viable model of how environmental justice implementation can be advanced through greater interagency cooperative efforts.

Regarding the second recommendation, Section 3 of this report presents the progress made by federal agencies in integrating environmental justice into policies and programs. In developing this recommendation, the NEJAC recognizes and complements these initial federal agency implementation efforts and encourages agencies to take implementation efforts to a higher level within their programs, such as integrating environmental justice protections and criteria into program design and evaluation.

Section 2 of this report begins to identify opportunities that exist under current environmental laws and statutory authorities to promote environmental justice, but the council notes that there is a broader universe of laws that have yet to be examined by agencies other than EPA. In its third recommendation, the NEJAC recognizes the potential within the current statutory basis to implement the requirements of the Executive Order.

APPENDIX A

INDIGENOUS PEOPLES SUBCOMMITTEE
OF THE
NATIONAL ENVIRONMENTAL JUSTICE ADVISORY COUNCIL

Recommendations Concerning Integration of Environmental Justice
in Federal Agency Programs

February 10, 2002

INTRODUCTION

There are some 556 federally recognized tribal governments in the United States, which includes some 223 Alaska Native villages.[1] Indian tribal governments possess a unique political and legal status in the United States. Tribes have long been recognized as separate sovereigns possessing broad inherent authority over their members and territories, however, tribes also are subject to applicable federal law. As governments, the relationship between federally recognized tribes and the federal government is described as "government-to-government" and, in 1994 and 2000, President Clinton directed each federal agency to operate within this relationship[2] and to maintain it through meaningful consultation and coordination with tribes (Tribal Consultation Policy).[3] Moreover, the federal government owes a special obligation, known as the trust responsibility, toward federally recognized Indian tribes to protect their status as self-governing entities and their property rights. The trust responsibility is based on treaties, statutes, executive orders, and the historical relations between the federal government and tribes. Significantly, it is this trust responsibility that distinguishes federally recognized tribes from all other ethnic and minority groups. Thus, it is the view of the Indigenous Peoples Subcommittee ("IPS") that these circumstances warrant the additional, specific recommendations set forth in this document.

At the time of the 1990 census, about 1.9 million persons living in the United States identified themselves as American Indians/Alaska Natives ("AI/ANs").[4] In 1993, the Bureau of Indian Affairs estimated that 1.2 million AI/ANs lived within Indian country[5] on lands reserved for their tribes as permanent homelands.[6] AI/ANs are particularly susceptible to health impacts from pollution due to their traditional and cultural uses of natural resources and, in fact, AI/AN "have greater exposure risks than the general population as a result of their dietary practices and unique cultures that embrace the environment."[7] Fishing, hunting, and gathering often are part of a spiritual, cultural, social, and economic lifestyle, and the survival of many AI/ANs depends on subsistence hunting, fishing, and gathering. In some instances, the right to engage in these activities is legally protected by treaty. Additionally, many AI/ANs also use water, plants, and animals in their traditional and religious practices and ceremonies. As a result, contamination of the water, soil, plants, and animals and the subsequent accumulation of these contaminants in the people through ingestion and contact[8] not only endangers the health of AI/ANs, but also threatens the well-being of their future generations[9] and undermines the cultural survival of tribes and Alaska Native villages.

Significantly, where such traditional, cultural, and subsistence activities are involved, federal and state environmental standards used to protect the general non-Indian/non-Native population may not afford tribes and Alaska Native villages adequate protection from environmental harm.[10] Although several of the major federal environmental laws have been amended to allow federally recognized tribes to assume primacy for certain programs,[11] to date, only a few tribes have Environmental Protection Agency- approved or -promulgated environmental programs.[12] Thus, it is the strong view of the IPS that federally recognized tribes and AI/ANs suffer a disproportionate burden of health consequences due to their exposure to pollutants and hazardous substances in the environment. This is particularly so for AI/AN infants and children.[13]

RECOMMENDATIONS

In developing recommendations for the Environmental Protection Agency (EPA) on how federal agencies are integrating environmental justice (EJ) into their policies, programs, and activities affecting federally-recognized tribes, the IPS has identified the following overarching principles that must be considered:

- Tribal Sovereignty

- Government-to-Government Relationship Between Tribes and the United States including its Agencies

- EPA Indian Policy for the Administration of Environmental Programs on Indian Reservations (Nov. 8, 1984), reaffirmed by EPA Administrator Christine Todd Whitman on July 11, 2001

- Tribal Consultation Policy

- Federal Trust Responsibility to Tribes and Alaska Native Villages

Based on the foregoing, the IPS makes the following recommendations specifically applicable to the integration of EJ within Indian country by EPA and other federal agencies:

1. **EPA and other federal agencies should better implement existing environmental and public health laws by improving capacity building for tribes and federal agencies.**

    A. Additional financial and technical resources and training for tribes and federal agencies are needed to enhance awareness and understanding of laws, regulations, Indian law principles, and policies applicable to tribes and Indian country (*e.g.*, federal trust responsibility, government-to-government working relationship, and tribal sovereignty).
    B. Federal agencies should work with each tribe to identify that tribe's needs and then take all appropriate steps to see that those needs are met, including but not limited to seeking support from Congress, reprogramming agency funds, and/or redirecting staff.
    C. The federal government should create a document showing how, who, and what resources exist to work with tribes in protecting their environment and public health and in providing for sound tribal economic development.
    D. Partnerships between federal agencies and tribal colleges should be increased to assist tribes in building their environmental and natural resource management and sustainable development capacities.
    E. Demographic information on the academic disciplines and placement of Native students among categories of higher education institutions should be obtained to determine the tribal community resources potentially available for capacity building.
    F. A list of non-federal funding should be developed as possible sources to supplement tribal projects and programs (*e.g.*, renewable energy).

2. **EPA and other federal agencies should encourage and enhance opportunities for interagency coordination to address tribal environmental, public health, and economic development needs.**

   A. Because federal environmental missions and resources are divided among and in some cases overlap between various agencies, EPA and other federal agencies should coordinate and pool available technical and financial resources to provide economic development, health, and environmental-related services, including environmental justice programs, to federally recognized tribes equitably, efficiently, and effectively. Towards this end, the Bureau of Indian Affairs, EPA, Department of Housing and Urban Development, and the Indian Health Service should appraise the usefulness and implementation of the national Memorandum of Understanding ("MOU")[14] and take appropriate steps to enhance and better promote interagency coordination and collaboration pertaining to the protection of health and the environment within Indian country and Alaska Native villages and the promotion of sustainable tribal economies.

   B. A list of federal agency contacts at the local/regional level should be developed and shared with tribes so they can encourage federal agencies to lead interagency coordination efforts.

   C. A federal tracking system, a diary of tribal EJ concerns, if you will, should be developed in order to help agencies better understand and collectively respond to tribal concerns and needs (*e.g.*, DOD's tracking system on its web page). Transparency is important.

   D. EPA should assert a leadership role among federal agencies in developing new financing mechanisms and leveraging all available resources to fund and implement environmental and health-related projects and economic development initiatives in Indian country and Alaska Native villages. To address existing fiscal limits on the delivery of federal services to tribes, EPA and other federal agencies should marshal all available means to ensure that sufficient funding is available to address tribal needs; *provided* that every effort simply must be made to eliminate continuing inequities in federal funding to address the alarmingly high levels of unmet environmental, health, and economic development needs of tribes (*e.g.*, limited BIA funding for environmental liabilities; funding and staffing of the Indian Health Service at only 34% of the level of need).

   E. The recommendations generated at the Albuquerque Federal Interagency Tribal EJ Roundtable meeting should be reviewed and efforts undertaken to implement Roundtable recommendations with additional input from tribes and tribal organizations.

3. **EPA and other federal agencies should enhance the federal government's efforts to protect the environment and public health of tribes and AI/ANs through the National Environmental Policy Act (NEPA).**

   A. Federal agencies must improve their abilities to work with tribes in properly evaluating impacts from proposed project on tribal interests and AI/ANs through the environmental assessment (EA) and environmental impact statement (EIS) processes of NEPA.

   B. Among other things, application of the NEPA process in and around Indian country and Alaska Native villages should address sustainability and long- and short-term impacts on subsistence activities and health (*e.g.*, land use may contaminate, impair, or destroy subsistence resources resulting in health problems such as diabetes, cancer, and developmental disorders).

C.   Federal agencies and applicants conducting EAs must deal with Section 106 of the National Historic Preservation Act at the beginning of the process, and tribes should be consulted at "purpose and need."

D.   EPA should support interested tribes financially and technically in exploring effective ways to explain and protect their individual homelands uses and to set reservation land use objectives, including but not limited to the development of a "Tribal Environmental Policy Act."

ENDNOTES

1.   "Federally recognized" means that these tribes and groups have a special legal relationship with the United States. Additionally, a number of tribes and indigenous groups do not have federally recognized status, although some of these tribes are state-recognized or are in the process of seeking federal recognition.

2.   See Executive Memorandum on Government-to-Government Relations with Native American Tribal Governments (April 29, 1994).

3.   See Executive Order No. 13084 (May 14, 1998). On November 6, 2000, President Clinton issued a new order strengthening the policy on tribal consultation. See Executive Order No. 13175 (Nov. 6, 2000).

4.   AI/ANs are among the fastest growing ethnic/minority populations in the nation. The 1990 census showed a 37.9% increase over the population of AI/ANs in the 1980 census. For additional facts and general information, see the Bureau of Indian Affairs' homepage at <http://www.doi.gov/bia/aitoday/q_and_a.html>.

5.   "Indian country," which includes reservations, dependent Indian communities, and Indian allotments, comprises approximately 53 million acres of land, much of which is found in remote areas of the nation. The term "Indian country" is defined by federal law as including "(a) all land within the limits of any Indian reservation under the jurisdiction of the United States Government, notwithstanding the issuance of any patent, and, including rights of way running through the reservation, (b) all dependent Indian communities . . . and (c) all Indian allotments, the Indian titles to which have not been extinguished, including rights-of-way running through the same."   See 18 U.S.C. § 1151.

6.   For additional facts and general information, see the Bureau of Indian Affairs' homepage at <http://www.doi.gov/bia/aitoday/q_and_a.html>.

7.   See "Focus on American Indian and Alaska Native Populations," published by the Agency for Toxic Substances and Disease Registry, at pages 1-2.

8.   For example, tribes near the Hanford Nuclear Reservation have been working with the Agency for Toxic Substances and Disease Registry to design health assessments focusing on exposure effects from food consumption and other activities. These tribes want to learn if the Hanford releases affect native food items and local materials used in tribal products like storage and cooking baskets, mats, and clothing. See "Focus on American Indian and Alaska Native Populations," published by the Agency for Toxic Substances and Disease Registry, at page 5. Tribes located in coastal northern California are concerned about the pesticide exposure of some 300 traditional basketmakers who gather their own materials from the forests and roadsides. Because a disproportionate number of American Indian residents in Humboldt County, California have been diagnosed with cancer, tribes believe studies are needed to determine the exact cause of such cases. See Chuck Striplen, Mutzun Oholone Tribe, "Native Subsistence in a Toxic Environment: A Tribal Viewpoint," at page 14, EPA's OPPTS Tribal News (Fall/Winter 1999-2000).

9.   A number of studies have shown that children are uniquely susceptible to pollution and contaminants. For example, since 1992, the Agency for Toxic Substances and Disease Registry has funded research in the Great Lakes states focusing on the health effects of high risk populations, including

American Indians, from persistent toxic substances found in fish. One study found that newborns born to mothers who consumed only 2.3 PCB-contaminated Great Lakes fish meals per month scored lower on the Neonatal Behavioral Assessment Scale. See "Focus on American Indian and Alaska Native Populations," published by the Agency for Toxic Substances and Disease Registry, at pages 2-3. Additionally, in Oklahoma, Indian children also suffer harm from their environment. The Tar Creek Superfund Site, a former lead and zinc mine, occupies 40 square miles within the boundaries of the former Quapaw Indian Reservation. Both the Quapaw Tribe's powwow grounds and campgrounds are contaminated from mine tailings, and the Environmental Protection Agency Region 6 reports that approximately 25% of the Quapaw children have elevated blood lead levels compared with a statewide average of 2%. See "U.S. Environmental Protection Agency Region 6 Environmental Justice Update," at page 7 (May 2000).

10.   See, e.g., City of Albuquerque v. Browner, 97 F.3d 415 (10th Cir. 1996), cert. denied, 118 S. Ct. 410 (1997) (upholding the Environmental Protection Agency's approval of the Pueblo of Isleta's water quality standards that were more stringent than the state water quality standards, and which included a ceremonial use standard).

11.   Since 1986, the Safe Drinking Water Act, Clean Water Act, and Clean Air Act have been amended to afford tribes substantially the same opportunities as states to assume responsibility for certain programs or purposes.

12.   For example, the Environmental Protection Agency recently reported that, as of July 13, 2000, only 15 tribes have Environmental Protection Agency-approved or -promulgated water quality standards and no tribes are authorized to administer the National Pollutant Discharge Elimination System or to establish Total Maximum Daily Loads. See 65 Fed. Reg. 43,585 (July 13, 2000).

13.   For example, a New York State Department of Health study of lactating women and their infants linked breast feeding and infant exposure to hazardous substances. This study compared PCB levels in the breast milk of Mohawk women who gave birth between 1986 and 1992 with a control group. The study found that although the PCB concentrations in the breast milk of Mohawk mothers decreased over time, their infants had urine PCB levels ten times higher than that of their mothers. See "Focus on American Indian and Alaska Native Populations," published by the Agency for Toxic Substances and Disease Registry, at pages 3-4. See also Winona Laduke, All Our Relations, Native Struggles for Land and Life, at 11-23 (1999).

14.   In June 1991, the Bureau of Indian Affairs, the Environmental Protection Agency, the Department of Housing and Urban Development, and the Indian Health Service signed a MOU, which recognizes that each agency has responsibilities and interests regarding the protection of human health and the environment as it relates to pollution control and prevention within Indian country and Alaska Native villages. This national MOU identifies areas of mutual interest, encourages coordination to promote the most effective and integrated use of the agencies' resources, and expressly anticipates that regional and area offices of the signatory agencies may want to develop more specific MOUs.

APPENDIX B

NEJAC Interagency EJ Implementation Workgroup Members

Eileen Gauna (Workgroup Co-Chair)
Professor, Southwestern University School of Law

Pat Wood (Workgroup Co-Chair)
Senior Manager, Federal Regulatory Affairs, Georgia Pacific Corporation

Richard Gragg
Associate Director, Environmental Science Institute, Florida A&M University

Robert Harris
Vice President, Environmental Affairs, Pacific Gas and Electric Company

Harold Mitchell
Director, Regenesis, Inc.

Mary Nelson
President, Bethel New Life, Inc.

Jane Stahl
Deputy Commissioner, Connecticut Department of Environmental Protection

Jana Walker
Attorney, Law Office of Jana L. Walker

Tseming Yang
Professor, Vermont Law School

www.ingramcontent.com/pod-product-compliance
Lightning Source LLC
Chambersburg PA
CBHW080908290526
45795CB00007BA/2459